S0-CFK-992

KAPLAN

Related Titles

AP U.S. History

AP U.S. Government and Politics

SAT Subject Test: U.S. History

KAPLAN

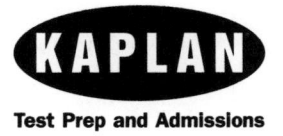

Test Prep and Admissions

U.S. History Flashcards Flip-O-Matic

Compiled by Jay Harmon

Simon & Schuster

NEW YORK · LONDON · SYDNEY · TORONTO

Kaplan Publishing
Published by SIMON & SCHUSTER
Rockefeller Center
1230 Avenue of the Americas
New York, NY 10020

Copyright © 2005 by Kaplan Publishing
All rights reserved. No part of this book may be reproduced or transmitted in any form or by any means, electronic or mechanical, including photocopying, recording, or by any information storage and retrieval system, without the written permission of the Publisher. Except where permitted by law.

Kaplan ® is a registered trademark of Kaplan, Inc.

SIMON & SCHUSTER and colophon are registered trademarks of Simon & Schuster, Inc.

Editorial Director: Jennifer Farthing
Project Editor: Anne Kemper
Production Manager: Michael Shevlin
Content Manager: Patrick Kennedy
Interior Page Layout: Baldur Gudbjornsson
Cover Design: Kam Tai

Manufactured in the United States of America.
Published simultaneously in Canada.

10 9 8 7 6 5 4 3 2 1

September 2005

ISBN-13: 978-0-7432-7378-7
ISBN-10: 0-7432-7378-8

For information regarding special discounts for bulk purchases, please contact Simon & Schuster Special Sales at 1-800-456-6798 or business@simonandschuster.com.

HOW TO USE THIS BOOK

Kaplan's *U.S. History Flashcards Flip-O-Matic* is perfectly designed to help you learn about 350 key U.S. history people, events, and concepts in a quick and easy way. The terms are arranged in approximate chronological order in 16 categories, from Exploration and Colonization to the present. Simply read the category (e.g., Revolutionary War Era) and term on the front of the flashcard; then flip to the back to see its definition and historical significance. Each term is numbered and definitions refer to related terms by number.

Terms marked with a ▼ nearly always appear on AP U.S. History and SAT Subject Test: U.S. History exams. The other terms often appear on these tests.

The following categories occur in this book, in chronological order.

Exploration and Colonization to 1754

Revolutionary War Era, 1754–1787

New Constitution and Government, 1787–1801

Jefferson Era, 1801–1824

Jackson Era, 1824–1844

Westward Expansion, 1820s–1850s

Buildup to the Civil War

Civil War and Reconstruction

Thirty Years of Change, 1865–1896

Theodore Roosevelt Era, 1898–1912

Wilson Era Through the 1920s, 1912–1929

The Great Depression and World War II, 1929–1945

Truman-Eisenhower Era, 1945–1961

Kennedy-Johnson Era, 1961–1969

Nixon-Carter Era, 1969–1981

Reagan to the Present, 1981–

Once you've mastered a particular term, clip or fold back the corner of the flashcard so that you can zip right by it on your next pass through the book. The flashcard book is packed with information—remember to flip the book over and flip through the other half!

Looking for still more AP and SAT Subject Test prep? Be sure to pick up Kaplan's *AP U.S. History* and *SAT Subject Test: U.S. History*, complete with full-length practice tests.

At the back of this book are blank pages for you to fill in with U.S. History terms you need to remember. Write the name of the person, event, or concept on the front of the card and the definition on the back. When you get to the end of the book, turn it upside down and go from back to front to create even more personalized flashcards.

Good luck!

1. COLUMBIAN EXCHANGE

On September 11, 2001 men in the al-Qaeda terrorist group hijacked four American passenger jets. Two flew into and destroyed the World Trade Center buildings in New York City. One crashed into the Pentagon in Washington, DC. The fourth plane crashed into the ground in Pennsylvania after an onboard struggle. Over 3000 people were killed in these four attacks.

Why important? 9/11 began a worldwide war against terrorism that has included U.S. military action in Afghanistan and Iraq.

Exploration and Colonization to 1754

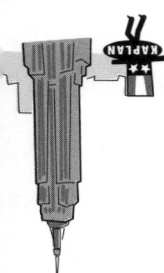

The Columbian Exchange was the introduction of plants, animals, and diseases from New World to Old and vice versa. Examples: From Old to New World: sugarcane, iron implements, cattle, horses and smallpox. From New to Old World: corn, tobacco, potatoes, and possibly syphilis. **Why important?** The Columbian exchange is the greatest legacy of Columbus's four voyages to the New World. Its consequences included the deaths of millions of Native Americans due to foreign disease.

350. 9/11

Reagan to the Present, 1981–

2. SIR WALTER RALEIGH

Reagan to the Present, 1981–

In the presidential election of 2000, President Clinton's vice president, Al Gore, challenged the vote count in the important electoral state of Florida and lost. The Supreme Court ruled in favor of the Republican candidate: George H.W. Bush's son, George W. Bush.

Why important? The 2000 election reminded many of the disputed presidential election of 1876 (#143).

Raleigh attempted the first English settlement of North America in 1587 at Roanoke Island, in present-day North Carolina. This was the famous "lost colony of Roanoke."

Why important? His colony failed but the English later succeeded in establishing other colonies in America.

349. 2000 ELECTION

Exploration and Colonization to 1754

3. ROBERT LASALLE

Reagan to the Present, 1981–

Population shifts continued moving West and South, mostly from the Northeastern part of America. Hispanics passed African Americans as the largest minority group. The divorce rate rose to about 50% of marriages and leveled off. The Baby Boomers (**#296**) passed middle age; concerns arose about the future of Social Security (**#268**). Women entered more jobs that had been filled by men in the areas of politics, corporate leadership, and the military (**#282, #329**).

Why important? Postwar migration patterns continued and women made significant social gains.

LaSalle claimed all the land drained by the Mississippi River for France in 1682. That's roughly from the Appalachians to the Rockies. He named this territory "Louisiana."

Why important? Conflicts arose with England during the French and Indian War (**#28**) over the northeastern boundaries of this claim, around present-day Pittsburgh.

348. TRENDS IN SOCIETY, 1970s–PRESENT

Reagan to the Present, 1981–

4. JAMESTOWN, VIRGINIA

Reagan to the Present, 1981–

Democratic President Bill Clinton was impeached by the Republican-majority House of Representatives for perjury and obstruction of justice in a sexual harassment case. Like Andrew Johnson (**#138**) Clinton was not convicted by the Senate.

Why important? These were the only two presidents to be impeached. The effectiveness of both suffered afterward.

Exploration and Colonization to 1754

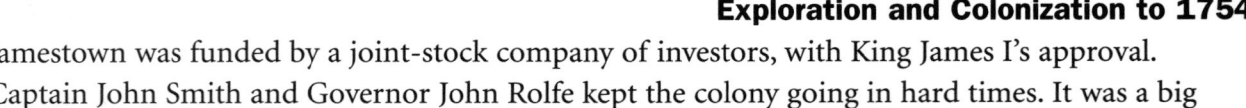

Jamestown was funded by a joint-stock company of investors, with King James I's approval. Captain John Smith and Governor John Rolfe kept the colony going in hard times. It was a big moneymaker: tobacco grown here was sold to England. It had the first representative assembly (House of Burgesses) and first Africans in America, both dating from 1619.

Why important? This was the first permanent English settlement in America (1607).

347. CLINTON IMPEACHMENT

Reagan to the Present, 1981–

The North American Free Trade Agreement (NAFTA) was a George H.W. Bush-era proposal approved by Congress and Bush's successor, President Bill Clinton. Taking effect in 1994, it eliminated import tariffs on goods traded between the United States, Mexico, and Canada. **Why important?** NAFTA's supporters say free trade has strengthened the economy by making American-made products cheaper in Mexico and Canada. Opponents, however, claim NAFTA resulted in "outsourcing" (loss of American jobs to cheaper foreign markets).

5. PLYMOUTH COLONY

Exploration and Colonization to 1754

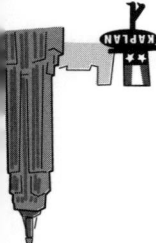

A group of 102 English Separatists ("Pilgrims") sailed to Massachusetts in 1620 aboard the *Mayflower*. William Bradford was governor. These Pilgrims had the first Thanksgiving dinner. Later, Plymouth merged with the Massachusetts Bay Colony (**#6**).

Why important? The Mayflower Compact, written by this group, was an early form of colonial government.

---

346. NAFTA

Reagan to the Present, 1981–

Exploration and Colonization to 1754

▼ 6. MASSACHUSETTS BAY COLONY

Reagan to the Present, 1981–

President George H.W. Bush organized a United Nations-approved military strike against Iraq after it invaded neighboring Kuwait in 1990. The American-led forces liberated Kuwait but Iraqi leader Saddam Hussein remained a regional threat.

Why important? 1) The overwhelming American victory reestablished the public's confidence in its military after the Vietnam War. 2) The Persian Gulf War foreshadowed another war with Iraq that broke out in 2003 **(#350).**

Exploration and Colonization to 1754

About 1000 English Puritans with the Massachusetts Bay Company set out for America and founded Boston around 1630. Their leader, John Winthrop, said the colony was a shining "city on a hill" (a Biblical reference). The Salem witch trials occurred in this colony at the end of the 1600s. **Why important?** This was the largest early colonial settlement.

---

345. PERSIAN GULF WAR (1991)

Reagan to the Present, 1981–

Exploration and Colonization to 1754

7. GREAT MIGRATION

Reagan to the Present, 1981–

Unlike Carter, Reagan played tough with the USSR, labeling it an "Evil Empire." He greatly increased defense spending; the Soviets went broke trying to keep up. In 1991, during George H.W. Bush's term, the USSR dissolved into several nations, communism fell in Eastern Europe, and the Cold War ended.

Why important? The world's two superpowers had threatened to destroy each other for over 40 years, but the Cold War ended quietly, with most formerly communist nations adopting capitalism and democracy.

Within 10 years of the settling of Boston, nearly 35,000 people emigrated from England to the Massachusetts Bay Colony.

Why important? This shows how popular a destination America was for many English, even early on.

344. REVIVED COLD WAR AND ITS END

Reagan to the Present, 1981–

8. EUROPEANS' TREATMENT OF NATIVES IN AMERICA

Reagan to the Present, 1981–

In the 1980s Congress ordered U.S. aid to anticommunist rebels (Contras) in Central America to be cut off; however, the Reagan administration attempted to help the Contras covertly with funds obtained through secret weapons sales to Iran.

Why important? Challenging communism around the world was a big part of Reagan's foreign policy (**#344**), but Congress determined the Reagan administration overstepped its authority in this case.

Exploration and Colonization to 1754

Conventional wisdom says the French generally treated natives the best, followed by the English, and then the Spanish.

Why important? In the French and Indian War (**#28**), most of the Indian warriors sided with France.

---

343. IRAN-CONTRA SCANDAL (1986–1988)

Reagan to the Present, 1981–

9. COLONY CHARTERS

Ferraro was Democratic presidential candidate Walter Mondale's running mate against Reagan in 1984.
Why important? Ferraro was the first woman from a major party to run for national office, although she and Mondale were not successful.

Three types of charters were issued to the American colonies by England's king. A charter was permission to form a new colony.

The three types were: 1) Corporate (a.k.a. joint-stock companies.) Example: Jamestown in the early days. 2) Royal or Crown, run directly by the king's government. Examples: New York, Connecticut. 3) Proprietary, financed and run by individuals. Examples: Maryland, Pennsylvania.

Why important? The 13 colonies developed differently over time, partly because of the diverse ways they were run.

342. GERALDINE FERRARO

▼ 10. TOLERATION ACT

Reagan to the Present, 1981–

Ronald Reagan's victory over Carter in the 1980 presidential election triggered a resurgence of conservatism in politics, labeled the "Reagan Revolution." Reagan contrasted with Carter by exuding an air of confidence and optimism and at the same time reviving Cold War rivalries with the Soviet Union (**#301**) after several years of détente (**#334**). He cut taxes to revive the economy, and he was the first president since Eisenhower (**#308**) to serve two full terms.

Why important? The Reagan era restored a lot of national pride that was lost after Vietnam (**#331, #333**) and Watergate (**#338**).

Maryland was founded (1634) by Lord Baltimore as a refuge for English Catholics. The colony's Toleration Act (1649) granted religious freedom to all Christians.

Why important? This was an early example of religious tolerance and of civil rights in America.

---

341. REAGAN REVOLUTION

Reagan to the Present, 1981–

Three key events emerged to define Carter's foreign-policy legacy. 1) He negotiated the Camp David Accords, the first peace treaty between Israel and Egypt (or any Arab nation). 2) He signed the Panama Canal Treaty promising to give control of the canal to Panama in 2000. 3) Most importantly, after the 1979 Iranian Revolution anti-American groups in Iran held 52 Americans hostage for over a year. Carter was unable to obtain freedom for them.

Why important? Carter's inability to resolve the Iran hostage crisis destroyed his chances for reelection in 1980.

---

11. BACON'S REBELLION

In Virginia (1676), Nathaniel Bacon, a farmer, led a rebellion against the policies of Governor William Berkeley. The rebels wanted farmer-friendly economic policies and protection from Indians. The rebellion collapsed when Bacon died of dysentery.

Why important? It showed sharp class differences that were developing in the colonies, and it was an early example of colonial resistance to British governance.

340. CARTER FOREIGN POLICY

Nixon-Carter Era, 1969–1981

12. INDENTURED SERVANTS

A Democrat and political outsider from Georgia, Carter defeated Ford in the 1976 presidential election. Carter portrayed a folksy, honest image that appealed to Americans after the Watergate scandal (**#338**). However, Carter faced difficulty getting his domestic agenda through Congress.

Why important? Though likeable, Carter lacked political acumen and his popularity declined over time.

These people worked for landowners for free for 4 to 7 years in exchange for passage to America. At the end of their servitude, workers were often given land of their own. The first Africans in Jamestown (#4) were indentured servants, but by the 1660s slavery was the norm there.

Why important? Many early settlers in Virginia and Maryland got their start in America as indentured servants.

339. JIMMY CARTER (1977–1981)

Nixon-Carter Era, 1969–1981

▼ 13. ANNE HUTCHINSON

Numerous scandals involving Nixon's 1972 reelection campaign led to his resignation in 1974. The most famous centered on the burglary of the Democratic election headquarters in Washington, DC's Watergate Hotel by men working for Nixon. Investigations by reporters led to Senate hearings, and a House committee voted to begin impeachment proceedings (**#138**). Rather than face impeachment, Nixon resigned and Vice President Gerald Ford became president.

Why important? The Watergate scandal marked Nixon's as one of the most corrupt presidencies, along with those of Grant (**#155**) and Harding (**#237**). Nixon was the only president to resign.

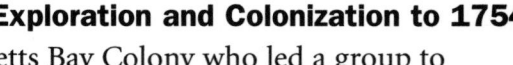

Hutchinson was a religious dissenter from the Massachusetts Bay Colony who led a group to Rhode Island following the example of an earlier dissenter, Roger Williams.

Why important? This was an early example of American dissent from authority and an example of political and spiritual leadership from a woman—very unusual for the time.

338. WATERGATE

Nixon-Carter Era, 1969–1981

14. FUNDAMENTAL ORDERS OF CONNECTICUT

President Nixon appealed to middle-class Americans who were dismayed by extremists in the youth culture (**#330**). In a televised speech (1969) Nixon asked the "great silent majority" to let its voice be heard as well. A large anti-counterculture movement began.

Why important? Conservatism, long in the political and social minority, reemerged as a powerful force in the United States.

Thomas Hooker led yet another group out of the Massachusetts Bay Colony in 1636, this time to Connecticut. The colony's constitution, the Fundamental Orders, established elected representative government (1639).

Why important? It was an early example of representative government and of dissention from unjust authority.

337. "SILENT MAJORITY"

Nixon-Carter Era, 1969–1981

Nixon-Carter Era, 1969–1981

In 1970 the first "Earth Day" called attention to the declining state of America's environment because of industrial pollution. In response, Nixon's administration started the federal Environmental Protection Agency to work with industry to reduce pollution.

Why important? The EPA has been an important factor in the overall improvement of America's environment over the subsequent decades.

---

15. HALFWAY COVENANT

Exploration and Colonization to 1754

Exploration and Colonization to 1754

By the 1660s New England churches began to lose influence, so they allowed members to take part in church services without a formal declaration of belief in Christ.

Why important? This showed the influence of the Puritans was weakening over time in New England as people became more prosperous.

336. EPA

Nixon-Carter Era, 1969–1981

16. NEW ENGLAND CONFEDERATION AND DOMINION OF NEW ENGLAND

Nixon-Carter Era, 1969–1981

The economic boom of the 1950s and '60s ended in October 1973. The Organization of Petroleum Exporting Countries (OPEC), comprised mainly of Arab nations in the Middle East, reduced its exports to the United States in retaliation for America's support of Israel in the Yom Kippur War. Rising gas prices led to inflation; at the same time, unemployment increased. This unprecedented condition was called *stagflation*. Even after OPEC lifted the embargo, the U.S. economy languished until the early 1980s.

Why important? Most Americans had assumed the economy always would be strong. This period proved them wrong.

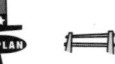

Exploration and Colonization to 1754

In 1643 the Plymouth, Massachusetts Bay, Connecticut, and New Haven colonies formed an alliance called the New England Confederation to defend themselves against Indian, French, and Dutch attacks. It lasted until 1684. In 1686, King James II created the Dominion of New England for similar reasons, but it was short-lived.

Why important? These set precedents for colonial cooperation, a useful idea in the French and Indian War (#28) and Revolutionary War.

335. ECONOMIC TRENDS IN THE 1970s

Nixon-Carter Era, 1969–1981

Nixon-Carter Era, 1969–1981

In 1972 Nixon began a thaw in the Cold War (**#301**) by flying to the USSR and communist China to meet with their leaders. Trade and military agreements were reached, including the Strategic Arms Limitation Treaty (SALT I) with the USSR. This era of improved cooperation with the communist bloc was called “détente.”

Why important? Nixon was a major Cold War supporter in the 1950s, so when he reached out to the USSR and communist China, it was taken very seriously.

17. NEW YORK

Exploration and Colonization to 1754

The Netherlands (Holland) originally settled present-day New York City, calling its colony "New Amsterdam." In 1664, England took over the colony and renamed it New York, but the Dutch settlers were treated with toleration.

Why important? New York City became a leading colonial port and New York a popular area of settlement.

334. DÉTENTE

Nixon-Carter Era, 1969–1981

Nixon-Carter Era, 1969–1981

Responding to public sentiment against the Vietnam War, Nixon had American troops gradually withdraw from Vietnam while U.S. military aid to South Vietnam continued. The last American combat soldier left in 1973; in 1975 the North attacked the South and won the war.

Why important? The United States lost a war for the first time. The results included a large migration of Vietnamese citizens to America and loss of U.S. prestige around the world.

Exploration and Colonization to 1754

18. HOLY EXPERIMENT

Exploration and Colonization to 1754

The Pennsylvania colony was established by a Quaker, William Penn. He provided religious toleration and a representative assembly. He considered these ideas a "holy experiment" and it worked. Pennsylvania became the most populous colony and Philadelphia the most populous city in America. **Why important?** Penn showed that getting along with others was a workable, popular, and profitable concept.

333. VIETNAMIZATION

Nixon-Carter Era, 1969–1981

North Vietnam launched the Tet Offensive. President Johnson did not run for reelection. Dr. Martin Luther King, Jr. and presidential candidate Robert F. Kennedy were assassinated. Race riots took place in Chicago, Detroit, and other cities. Violence between protesters and police broke out outside the Democratic National Convention in Chicago. Republican Richard Nixon won the presidential election.

Why important? After the Tet Offensive, a majority of Americans opposed the Vietnam War. Nixon slowly pulled U.S. troops out of Vietnam. After the assassinations and other events above, many feared the nation was headed toward anarchy.

19. JAMES OGLETHORPE

Oglethorpe founded Georgia, the 13th of the 13 colonies, as a haven for the poor and oppressed. However, he banned drinking, gambling, and slavery, and the colony languished until the English government took over.

Why important? Georgia was a buffer between Spanish Florida and the English Carolinas. This was the first of many attempts to establish a utopian society in America (#75).

---

332. 1968

The Kennedy-Johnson Era, 1961–1969

Exploration and Colonization to 1754

20. MERCANTILISM

The Kennedy-Johnson Era, 1961–1969

Starting in the late 1950s and ending in the mid-'70s, the United States sent aid to South Vietnam in its fight against communist North Vietnam and South Vietnamese citizens who favored communism. In 1965 the Gulf of Tonkin Resolution sent U.S. combat soldiers to take full part in the war.

Why important? The Vietnam War was the most divisive in American history and the first the United States lost. Its political and social repercussions were felt for decades after it ended.

This European economic policy saw colonies as an important source of raw materials for the mother country's benefit, and little else. Colonies were supposed to buy finished goods from the mother country. **Why important?** This policy by the English government often angered the colonists, ultimately leading to the American Revolution.

▲ 331. VIETNAM WAR (1957–1975)

The Kennedy-Johnson Era, 1961–1969

▼ 21. NAVIGATION ACTS

The Kennedy-Johnson Era, 1961–1969

The "Baby Boom" (**#296**) children of the late 1940s through the 1950s were the teenagers of the 1960s. Businesses discovered this group's buying power and began to focus on the youth market in automobiles, fashion, and the arts. Music was an especially strong market for the culture.

Why important? Appealing to the young is an even more important part of advertising today.

These were English rules for colonial trade, made to promote mercantilism (**#20**). Trade of certain "enumerated goods" from the colonies was supposed to go only to England, like tobacco. Over time new Navigation Acts expanded the list to almost everything the colonies produced. This angered colonial merchants like John Hancock.

Why important? Resentment built up in the colonies over restrictive trading regulations. Lots of smuggling to and from France and Holland occurred, which angered the English.

330. YOUTH CULTURE

The Kennedy-Johnson Era, 1961–1969

22. TRIANGULAR TRADE

The modern women's rights movement of the 1960s and '70s came about after the publication of Betty Friedan's book *The Feminine Mystique* (1963). In 1966 the National Organization for Women formed to promote career opportunities as well as social and political equality for women. Its most famous leader was Gloria Steinem.

Why important? Like the civil rights movement (**#325**) that promoted equality for African Americans, the women's rights movement made Americans aware of social, economic, and political inequities that women faced.

Exploration and Colonization to 1754

This refers to the general sea route across the Atlantic used to transport goods and slaves between the New World, Europe, and Africa. Raw materials traveled from America to Europe, manufactured goods from Europe to Africa, and slaves from Africa to America.

Why important? It shows the economic interdependence of three continents in colonial times.

▲ 329. WOMEN'S RIGHTS MOVEMENT

The Kennedy-Johnson Era, 1961–1969

Exploration and Colonization to 1754

23. MIDDLE PASSAGE

The Kennedy-Johnson Era, 1961–1969

Under Chief Justice Earl Warren, the U.S. Supreme Court ruled on *Brown v. Board of Education* (#315) in 1954, *Gideon v. Wainwright* (those accused can have a court-appointed attorney) in 1963, and *Miranda v. Arizona* (those accused must have their rights read to them by police) in 1966, among others.

Why important? Warren led the court during the 1950s and '60s, its most activist era, especially in the area of individual rights.

This was the route slave ships traveled across the Atlantic from Africa to the New World. Africans were often chained together and treated no better than animals. Over 90% of the Africans who survived the Middle Passage worked on Caribbean or South American plantations. Less than 10% went to North America.

Why important? It shows how far New World plantation owners were willing to go for cheap labor and how inhumane the slave trade was.

328. WARREN COURT (1953–1969)

The Kennedy-Johnson Era, 1961–1969

24. COLONIAL ECONOMIC TRENDS

The Kennedy-Johnson Era, 1961–1969

The Civil Rights Act of 1964 made segregation illegal in public places such as bus stations, movie theaters, hotels, and restaurants. The 24th Amendment (1964) made poll taxes illegal. The 1965 Voting Rights Act ended literacy tests.

Why important? These new laws were the most comprehensive and effective civil rights legislation since the Reconstruction era (#131).

Exploration and Colonization to 1754

New England colonies (CT, RI, MA, NH, VT) had small farms but excelled in shipbuilding, fishing, trading, and producing rum. Middle colonies (NY, NJ, PA, DE) produced wheat on larger farms and had large port cities like New York and Philadelphia. Southern colonies (MD, VA, NC, SC, GA) grew tobacco on large plantations and corn and rice on smaller farms. These colonies had the most slaves by far. The only city with a large population was Charleston, South Carolina. **Why important?** The environment—climate and soil—was a major factor in the different development of the colonies. People developed different attitudes about religion, government, and slavery, with enormous implications for future decades.

327. CIVIL RIGHTS ACT OF 1964

The Kennedy-Johnson Era, 1961–1969

Exploration and Colonization to 1754

25. THE GREAT AWAKENING

The Kennedy-Johnson Era, 1961–1969

President Kennedy was assassinated on November 22, 1963, and Vice President Lyndon Johnson became president. Johnson pushed Kennedy's education, Medicare, Medicaid, and civil rights legislation through Congress, claimed these domestic programs as his own, and called them the Great Society.

Why important? The Great Society was Johnson's version of Franklin Roosevelt's New Deal (#251), this time including civil rights. However, the ever-growing Vietnam War meant that funds for some Great Society programs were limited, turning many liberal Democrats against Johnson.

Exploration and Colonization to 1754

A religious revival occurred all over the colonies beginning in the 1730s. Jonathan Edwards was one famous evangelist who preached with great zeal. Belonging to a particular denomination was now not as important as having a personal relationship with God.

Why important? The Great Awakening had a unifying effect on Americans since it was something everyone experienced or at least knew about. It also changed Americans' views of religious and later, political, authority.

326. GREAT SOCIETY

The Kennedy-Johnson Era, 1961–1969

Exploration and Colonization to 1754

26. BENJAMIN FRANKLIN

The Kennedy-Johnson Era, 1961–1969

On August 28, 1963, between 200,000 and 500,000 activists and supporters gathered in Washington, DC to promote civil-rights legislation and racial harmony. Dr. Martin Luther King, Jr. (**#318**) gave his famous "I have a dream" speech. In 1964, Dr. King won the Nobel Peace Prize for his nonviolent promotion of racial equality in America.

Why important? The March on Washington was broadcast on TV and radio around the nation and eventually the world, and it was a turning point in the civil rights movement.

Franklin was America's first Renaissance man—someone active in many different fields. He was a writer, publisher, philanthropist, politician, scientist, inventor, U.S. ambassador to France, and editor of the Declaration of Independence. He published *Poor Richard's Almanac*, famous for its advice and witty sayings.

Why important? As the first American famous in Europe, Franklin brought about a new level of respect for Americans in Europeans' eyes.

325. MARCH ON WASHINGTON

The Kennedy-Johnson Era, 1961–1969

In October 1962 the USSR installed rockets with nuclear warheads in Cuba that were aimed at the United States. The United States found out and, citing the Monroe Doctrine (**#68**), told the Soviets to withdraw the missiles. Through the UN Security Council (**#294**), secret diplomacy, and clever military strategy, the United States got the USSR to remove the missiles.

Why important? This was the closest the two superpowers came to global war, and Kennedy's finest hour.

---

27. ZENGER LIBEL CASE

Exploration and Colonization to 1754

In 1735, New York publisher John Peter Zenger was put on trial for writing unpleasant things about the colony's governor. The jury decided Zenger had written the truth so he was not punished.

Why important? The case established a tradition—later to become law—in America that didn't exist in England: freedom of the press.

▲ 324. CUBAN MISSILE CRISIS

The Kennedy-Johnson Era, 1961–1969

Revolutionary War Era, 1754–1787

28. FRENCH AND INDIAN WAR

The Kennedy-Johnson Era, 1961–1969

After World War II the German city of Berlin was divided into communist East and capitalist West sectors. In 1961 the communists built a concrete wall around West Berlin to stop East Berlin residents from fleeing their sector. In 1963 President Kennedy famously visited the Berlin Wall.

Why important? The Berlin Wall was the most famous symbol of the Cold War. It stood from 1961 until 1989.

Revolutionary War Era, 1754–1787

The English and French fought over control of most of North America east of the Mississippi River from 1754 to 1763. France had a greater number of Indians on its side. The principal area of dispute was the northern Ohio River valley, focusing on the French Fort Duquesne (Pittsburgh). George Washington gained a lot of military experience in this war.

Why important? The British won, gaining Canada and all the land east of the Mississippi River.

323. BERLIN WALL

The Kennedy-Johnson Era, 1961–1969

Revolutionary War Era, 1754–1787

29. ALBANY PLAN OF UNION

The Kennedy-Johnson Era, 1961–1969

In April 1961 Kennedy attempted to overthrow Cuba's communist dictator, Fidel Castro, with a CIA-led invasion force of exiled Cuban citizens. The invasion was a complete failure. **Why important?** 1) Soviet leaders assumed Kennedy was weak on foreign policy. 2) Castro received increased aid from the USSR.

Revolutionary War Era, 1754–1787

During the French and Indian War, delegates from 7 colonies met to consider Benjamin Franklin's (#26) plan to unite for a common defense. The plan wasn't approved because arguments over sharing powers arose among the colonies.

Why important? Like the New England Confederation (#16), the Albany Plan of Union created a template for future colonial unity during the American Revolution.

322. BAY OF PIGS INVASION

The Kennedy-Johnson Era, 1961–1969

The Kennedy-Johnson Era, 1961–1969

John F. Kennedy, a Democrat from Massachusetts, won the 1960 presidential election. He called his domestic program the New Frontier. It included increased federal aid to education, civil rights legislation, and federal healthcare support for the aged (Medicare) and the poor (Medicaid). It also cut taxes.

Why important? Most of the New Frontier proposals were not approved by Congress until after Kennedy's assassination.

30. SALUTARY NEGLECT

Revolutionary War Era, 1754–1787

Revolutionary War Era, 1754–1787

For much of the colonial era England chose to look the other way while Americans ignored the Navigation Acts (**#21**). This unofficial policy was called *salutary neglect.*

Why important? After the French and Indian War, England needed money to protect the colonies and pay war debts, so it began to enforce its long-ignored laws—this angered many Americans.

321. NEW FRONTIER

The Kennedy-Johnson Era, 1961–1969

Revolutionary War Era, 1754–1787

▼ 31. PROCLAMATION OF 1763

The Kennedy-Johnson Era, 1961–1969

Vice President Richard Nixon and Senator John F. Kennedy held the first-ever presidential debates in 1960, and they were televised.

Why important? The Nixon-Kennedy debates showed the political importance of portraying a good image on television. Most people who listened on the radio thought Nixon won the debates; TV viewers thought Kennedy did.

Revolutionary War Era, 1754–1787

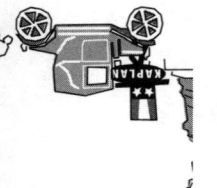

To protect the colonies from Indian attacks, England ruled that no Americans could move west of the Appalachian Mountains and that trading with Indians was forbidden.

Why important? This new law infuriated many Americans and thousands went west anyway: another example of American defiance that ultimately led to the revolution.

320. NIXON-KENNEDY DEBATES

The Kennedy-Johnson Era, 1961–1969

32. GRENVILLE PROGRAM

In 1961 Eisenhower famously warned Americans of the growing power of the "military-industrial complex," meaning he feared the arms race for conventional and nuclear weapons in the Cold War (#301) might be getting out of hand.

Why important? Eisenhower was a career military man, so his warning came as a surprise but it also carried a lot of clout.

Revolutionary War Era, 1754–1787

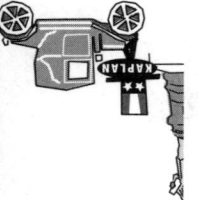

To raise money to defend Britain's North American possessions, Prime Minister George Grenville imposed new taxes on the colonies. The Sugar Act (1764) taxed sugar, and it tightened smuggling laws. The Quartering Act (1765) required colonists to feed and shelter British soldiers. Most famously, the Stamp Act (1765) put a direct tax (a tax added at the time of purchase) on printed paper. These were the first taxes that England required American consumers to pay directly from their pockets. **Why important?** Americans such as Samuel Adams organized groups in reaction, most famously the Sons of Liberty. Boycotts of British goods began. England quickly repealed the Stamp Act, but in the Declaratory Act it told the colonies they still were subject to the king's laws.

319. EISENHOWER'S FAREWELL ADDRESS

Truman and Eisenhower, 1945–1961

33. TOWNSHEND ACTS

In 1955, Dr. Martin Luther King, Jr. led the Montgomery, Alabama bus boycott begun by Rosa Parks (**#316**). In 1957 Dr. King, a minister, formed the Southern Christian Leadership Conference (SCLC) to inspire African-American church leaders in the South to use peaceful action against segregation. The peak of his influence came with the 1963 March on Washington (**#325**).

Why important? Dr. King was America's greatest civil rights leader in the 20th century.

Revolutionary War Era, 1754–1787

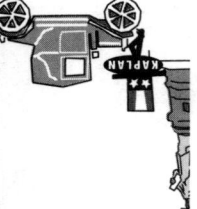

The Grenville program (**#32**) failed but England still needed money to defend the American colonies, so an indirect tax was placed on popular items like tea, glass, and paper. (Indirect taxes were included in the "sticker price" of an item). The Townshend Acts also allowed "writs of assistance" giving officials power to search anywhere for smuggling. This angered smugglers like John Hancock. Samuel Adams protested the new laws and promoted boycotts of English goods. **Why important?** The English backed down again and repealed most of these taxes. Many Americans were encouraged, thinking whenever they protested Britain would back down. This led to false assumptions about England's desire to enforce its laws.

▲ 318. DR. MARTIN LUTHER KING, JR.

Truman and Eisenhower, 1945–1961

Truman and Eisenhower, 1945–1961

The National Aeronautics and Space Administration (NASA) was founded during Eisenhower's second term. It came in response to the Soviet Union's launch of the first space satellite, Sputnik, in 1958.

Why important? The U.S. entry into the "space race" was an example of peaceful Cold War competition. It led to the Apollo moon program of the 1960s.

34. BOSTON MASSACRE

Revolutionary War Era, 1754–1787

Revolutionary War Era, 1754–1787

In 1770, eight British soldiers fired on a crowd, killing five Bostonians, most likely in self-defense. The most famous of the Americans killed was of African descent, Crispus Attucks.

Why important? Though his cousin John Adams defended the soldiers in their trial, Samuel Adams used the event to ratchet up colonial suspicion of British rule.

---

317. NASA

Truman and Eisenhower, 1945–1961

Truman and Eisenhower, 1945–1961

1947: Jackie Robinson became the first African American to play major-league baseball.

1948: Truman ordered the U.S. Armed Forces to integrate.

1954: *Brown v. Board of Education* (**#315**)

1955: Rosa Parks began the Montgomery, Alabama bus boycott to protest segregated bus systems in the South.

1957: Eisenhower sent U.S. soldiers to Little Rock, Arkansas to enforce integration of Central High School.

Why important? The 1960s civil rights movement (**#318, #325**) would not have occurred had these important events not come first.

---

35. BOSTON TEA PARTY

In 1773, Sons of Liberty dressed as Indians dumped 342 chests of tea off English cargo ships into Boston Harbor to protest another new tax.
Why important? This led to the Intolerable Acts (**#36**).

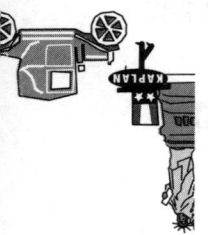

316. CIVIL RIGHTS ACTIVITIES IN THE TRUMAN-EISENHOWER ERA

Truman and Eisenhower, 1945–1961

Revolutionary War Era, 1754–1787

36. INTOLERABLE ACTS

Truman and Eisenhower, 1945–1961

In 1954, the Supreme Court ruled that the "separate but equal" provision of *Plessy v. Ferguson* (#158) was unconstitutional and ordered that public schools be desegregated "with all deliberate speed."

Why important? This is the most important civil rights case of the 20th century. It led to the civil rights movement of the 1960s (**#318, #325**).

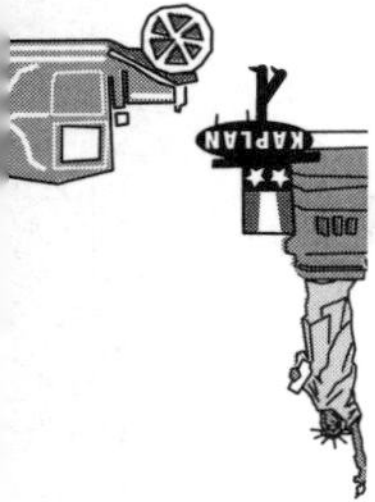

To punish Boston for the Tea Party (**#35**), Parliament passed the Coercive Acts (1774), a series of measures designed to enforce British authority over the colonies. Samuel Adams labeled them the Intolerable Acts. The acts closed Boston's port, reduced the power of the Massachusetts legislature, put land in the Ohio River Valley under Canadian control, forced colonists to house British soldiers, and prevented local administration of justice in Massachusetts.

Why important? Americans united against what they saw as unfair treatment and 12 colonies sent delegates to the First Continental Congress (**#37**).

315. BROWN V. BOARD OF EDUCATION, TOPEKA, KANSAS

Truman and Eisenhower, 1945–1961

37. FIRST CONTINENTAL CONGRESS

Truman and Eisenhower, 1945–1961

After some tense years of the Cold War (**#301**), in 1960 Eisenhower met with USSR Premier Nikita Khruschev in Geneva, Switzerland to talk cooperation. A "thaw" in the Cold War began. This ended at the end of Eisenhower's second term when an American U-2 spy jet was shot down over the Soviet Union.

Why important? The Geneva talks gave both sides hope that confrontation was not inevitable. Unfortunately, the U-2 Incident renewed old tensions.

Revolutionary War Era, 1754–1787

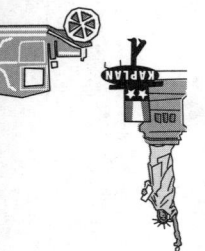

Twelve colonies (not Georgia) sent delegates to Philadelphia in 1774 to organize against what they saw as harsh treatment by the English. The Adams cousins (John and Samuel), Patrick Henry, and George Washington were among the participants. They resolved to resist the Intolerable Acts through more boycotts and to ask the king to restore the colonists' rights as English citizens. They pledged to meet again in a year if conditions didn't improve to their satisfaction.

Why important? This was the first large-scale sign of American unity against English colonial policy. The English government sent more troops to Massachusetts to keep order, which only angered the colonists more.

314. SPIRIT OF GENEVA

Truman and Eisenhower, 1945–1961

38. BATTLES OF LEXINGTON AND CONCORD

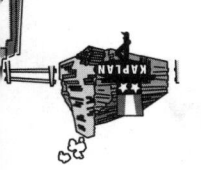

George Kennan of Truman's State Department developed this concept and that of containment (**#303**). Eisenhower declared his support for the Domino Theory in 1954. The idea was that if one country in Southeast Asia (namely, Vietnam) fell to communism, a chain reaction of communist takeovers would occur throughout Asia, and perhaps across the Pacific, eventually threatening even the United States.

Why important? The Domino Theory was a prevailing reason for U.S. involvement in Southeast Asia for 20 years.

Revolutionary War Era, 1754–1787

In April 1775, the British army in Boston marched out of town to Concord seeking military supplies that angry colonists had stored. Between Boston and Concord, at the town of Lexington, American militia called “Minute Men” exchanged musket fire with the British but ran off. Continuing to Concord, the British soldiers were forced to turn back by even more Minute Men. By the time they reached Boston again, 250 of the British “redcoats” were dead or wounded.

Why important? The “shot heard ‘round the world” at Lexington began the American Revolution.

▲ 313. DOMINO THEORY

Truman and Eisenhower, 1945–1961

39. SECOND CONTINENTAL CONGRESS

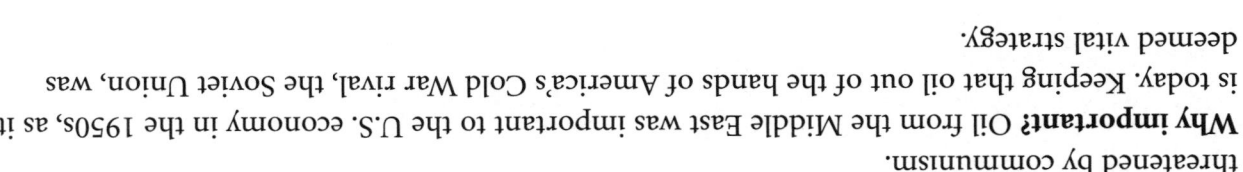

Eisenhower applied the Truman Doctrine of containment (#303) to the Middle East. The U.S. government promised military and economic aid to any country in that region that was threatened by communism.

Why important? Oil from the Middle East was important to the U.S. economy in the 1950s, as it is today. Keeping that oil out of the hands of America's Cold War rival, the Soviet Union, was deemed vital strategy.

Revolutionary War Era, 1754–1787

Clearly, relations between the American colonies and the English government had not improved in the year since the First Continental Congress (**#37**). Representatives from all 13 colonies showed up for the Second (1775). They called for volunteers from all the colonies to fight. Hedging their bets, the delegates also sent the “Olive Branch Petition” to the king, asking for peace and proper treatment as loyal British citizens.

Why important? The Second Continental Congress made George Washington commander-in-chief of the Continental Army.

312. EISENHOWER DOCTRINE

Truman and Eisenhower, 1945–1961

Eisenhower's secretary of state, John Foster Dulles, said because the United States had superiority in nuclear weapons it could afford to push the USSR to the brink of war if necessary. Because the USSR knew it would lose, it would always back down.

Why important? Under Eisenhower, combative Cold War (**#301**) rhetoric continued.

40. BATTLE OF BUNKER HILL

In June 1775 near Boston, in one of the bloodiest battles of the American Revolution, British soldiers attacked a Patriot (American) cannon emplacement.

Why important? The first real battle of the Revolutionary War was a tactical victory for the British but a moral one for the Americans, who showed they could fight just as well as the greatest army in the world.

311. BRINKSMANSHIP

Truman and Eisenhower, 1945–1961

41. THOMAS PAINE

Truman and Eisenhower, 1945–1961

Shortly after World War II, inflation and strikes returned and so did fears of another Great Depression (**#246**); however, the American economy boomed and inflation flattened throughout the 1950s.

Why important? The 15 years after World War II saw the greatest growth of the American economy in history.

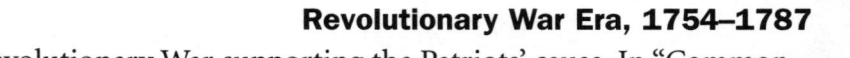

Revolutionary War Era, 1754–1787

Paine wrote literature during the Revolutionary War supporting the Patriots' cause. In "Common Sense" he declared it was time for the colonies to create their own nation, separate from England. In "The Crisis" he encouraged Americans to remain loyal to the Patriot effort, even through difficult times.

Why important? Paine was a powerful writer who influenced American public opinion regarding independence and the Revolutionary War cause.

---

310. ECONOMIC TRENDS IN THE TRUMAN-EISENHOWER ERA

Truman and Eisenhower, 1945–1961

42. DECLARATION OF INDEPENDENCE

One of Eisenhower's domestic achievements was the introduction of an efficient highway system that crisscrossed America. It was justified as a means to rapidly transport military supplies in case of war.

Why important? The interstate system became a major reason for the tremendous growth of suburbs and of travel in the United States.

Revolutionary War Era, 1754–1787

In July 1776, the Second Continental Congress (**#39**) declared the united colonies free of British rule. Thomas Jefferson was the chief author of the document, which included a list of complaints against British tyranny and an official declaration of war.

Why important? This formal break with Great Britain naturally holds a central position in American history.

309. INTERSTATE HIGHWAY SYSTEM

Truman and Eisenhower, 1945–1961

Revolutionary War Era, 1754–1787

43. TORIES

Truman and Eisenhower, 1945–1961

Commander of all Allied forces in Europe, Eisenhower served two terms as president of the United States (1953–1961). He was the first Republican elected president since Hoover (**#248**).

Why important? Eisenhower portrayed a calm father-figure persona in the 1950s, yet he led America during an era of great social change and international challenges.

Revolutionary War Era, 1754–1787

About one third of the colonists were Patriots, supporting independence, one third were neutral, and one third supported England. Members of the last group were the Tories or Loyalists, and many fought in battles on England's side.

Why important? The American colonists were not as united as many people think.

308. DWIGHT EISENHOWER

Truman and Eisenhower, 1945–1961

44. BATTLE OF SARATOGA

China became a communist nation in 1949 and in 1950 the Korean War started. These examples of communist expansion prompted Congress to hold the House Un-American Activities Committee, and separately, Senator Joe McCarthy held hearings seeking—and sometimes, creating—evidence of communist spies in the U.S. State Department and the Army. Julius and Ethel Rosenberg were convicted of giving atomic bomb secrets to the USSR, and executed. **Why important?** The first Red Scare (#233) and the second reflected the uncertainty that accompanied great social and international changes after both world wars.

Revolutionary War Era, 1754–1787

The turning point of the American Revolution, this battle took place in New York in 1777. The British army was utterly defeated by the Patriots.

Why important? The victory persuaded France to help the Americans against England. Foreign assistance from Spain and Holland arrived as well, giving the Americans a greatly needed boost in supplies and men.

---

307. SECOND RED SCARE

Truman and Eisenhower, 1945–1961

Truman and Eisenhower, 1945–1961

Korea was divided after World War II into communist North Korea and democratic South Korea. In 1950, North Korea invaded South Korea. The United Nations sent American-dominated forces to contain North Korea's aggression. In 1953 a peace settlement established boundaries near their original location.

Why important? While the war ended in a stalemate, it was a victory for the Truman Doctrine of containment (#303).

---

45. BATTLE OF YORKTOWN

Revolutionary War Era, 1754–1787

In Virginia in 1781, Washington defeated the British with help from French land and sea forces.

Why important? This was the last major battle of the Revolutionary War.

---

306. KOREAN WAR (1950–1953)

Truman and Eisenhower, 1945–1961

Revolutionary War Era, 1754–1787

46. TREATY OF PARIS (1783)

Truman and Eisenhower, 1945–1961

The North Atlantic Treaty Organization (est. 1949) was a U.S.-led military alliance designed to protect Western Europe from Soviet aggression. The Soviet Union countered with an alliance of its own, the Warsaw Pact (est. 1955).

Why important? NATO was another example of the Truman Doctrine. Despite the fall of the USSR in 1991 NATO still exists.

Revolutionary War Era, 1754–1787

In the treaty that ended the American Revolution, England recognized the independence of the United States and its western boundary at the Mississippi River.

Why important? America gained independence from the British for good.

---

305. NATO

Truman and Eisenhower, 1945–1961

47. ARTICLES OF CONFEDERATION

Truman and Eisenhower, 1945–1961

Western Europe struggled to recover from World War II and communists gained influence there. To counter this trend, the U.S. government gave billions of dollars to Western European nations for building and road construction between 1948 and 1951. In a few years, Western Europe's economy was booming.

Why important? This was an enormously successful example of containment (#303).

Revolutionary War Era, 1754–1787

The first constitution of the United States, it existed from 1776 to 1788. Strengths: 1) The United States won the war under this constitution. 2) The Land Ordinance of 1785 and the Northwest Ordinance of 1787 made rules for the addition of states in the future. Weaknesses: 1) There was no strong chief executive. 2) No national courts existed. 3) Congress had no power to tax.

Why important? Set the template for the next, and permanent, U.S. Constitution.

Truman and Eisenhower, 1945–1961

304. MARSHALL PLAN

48. SHAYS'S REBELLION

Truman and Eisenhower, 1945–1961

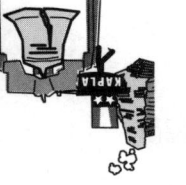

The Truman Doctrine (1947), or "containment," said the United States and its allies would work not to eliminate communism worldwide, but rather to keep the USSR from spreading its influence. The first successful test was the Berlin Airlift. The USSR tried to cut off western-controlled West Berlin in Germany but the United States and Britain flew supplies in by airplane for a year and the USSR backed off.

Why important? The Truman Doctrine was eventually applied worldwide and was America's default foreign policy regarding the USSR until 1991.

Revolutionary War Era, 1754–1787

In 1786, Daniel Shays led a rebellion of Massachusetts farmers against government economic policies (**#54**).

Why important? The rebellion was stopped, but many perceived a weakness in the U.S. government under the Articles of Confederation. If the national government were strong, they argued, people like Shays would be too intimidated to start trouble in the first place.

---

303. TRUMAN DOCTRINE

Truman and Eisenhower, 1945–1961

New Constitution and Government, 1787–1801

49. ANNAPOLIS CONVENTION

Truman and Eisenhower, 1945–1961

In a speech in Missouri in 1946, former British Prime Minister Winston Churchill said Soviet-dominated Eastern Europe lay behind an "iron curtain" of communist oppression.

Why important? This became one of the most famous expressions of the Cold War era and is a famous example of the combative rhetoric of that time. In another famous example, in the 1950s, Soviet leader Khruschev told the United States, "We will bury you."

New Constitution and Government, 1787–1801

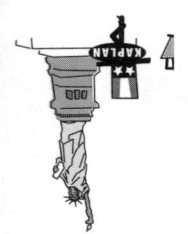

After a few years under the Articles of Confederation (#47) it became clear to many people that they weren't effective enough. Delegates met in Annapolis, Maryland in 1786 and agreed to revise and strengthen the Articles at another meeting in Philadelphia.

Why important? The Annapolis Convention led to the Constitutional Convention of 1787.

302. IRON CURTAIN

Truman and Eisenhower, 1945–1961

▼ 50. CONSTITUTIONAL CONVENTION (1787)

Truman and Eisenhower, 1945–1961

This term refers to the era of hostility between the United States and USSR from the late 1940s to early 1990s. Each of these superpowers amassed allies and weapons in an effort to counter the other. The Korean War (#306) and Vietnam War (#331) were Cold War struggles.

Why important? The Cold War was the main foreign policy concern of every president from Truman to George H.W. Bush.

New Constitution and Government, 1787–1801

George Washington, Ben Franklin (**#26**), James Madison, and Alexander Hamilton were among the delegates from 12 states (not Rhode Island) who attended the Constitutional Convention. They created an improved national government. The executive branch was strengthened, a national judicial system was established, and Congress received the power to tax. The "Great Compromise" expanded Congress to two houses: the Senate had two members from each state, and the House of Representatives had representation based on population. According to the "Three-Fifths Compromise," for every five slaves noted in the census, three counted toward representation in the House. A Bill of Rights was added after the next Congress took power in 1789.

Why important? The U.S. Constitution is the oldest document in the world that establishes a democratic republic.

---

301. COLD WAR

Truman and Eisenhower, 1945–1961

51. FEDERALISTS VS. ANTI-FEDERALISTS

This was Truman's version of the New Deal (**#251**). After a surprise win in the 1948 presidential election, Truman set an ambitious domestic agenda that included an increase in the minimum wage (**#271**) and Social Security payments (**#268**), as well as civil rights legislation (**#316**).

Why important? All presidents since Franklin D. Roosevelt dealt with the legacy of the New Deal by implementing their own domestic programs.

New Constitution and Government, 1787–1801

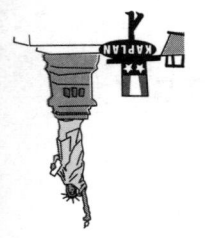

Federalists supported the upgraded powers the new Constitution gave the national government, while Anti-Federalists wanted the states to continue to have more power than the federal government. The Federalists won when the Constitution was ratified, but the Anti-Federalists got their way with the inclusion of the Bill of Rights, which limited the powers of the national government. The Washington-Adams presidencies are called the Federalist Era.

Why important? The arguments over the powers of the U.S. government led to the formation of the two-party political system.

▲ 300. FAIR DEAL

Truman and Eisenhower, 1945–1961

52. *THE FEDERALIST PAPERS*

Truman and Eisenhower, 1945–1961

After Roosevelt's presidency, Republicans were generally pro-business and Democrats pro-labor. When Republicans retook the House and Senate in 1947, they passed the Taft-Hartley Act to limit the power of labor unions. Among other things, it outlawed the practice of requiring workers to join a union. It also gave the president power to delay a strike that might endanger national security.

Why important? The Taft-Hartley Act was controversial in the 1950s but still exists.

To convince voters in New York to vote for the new Constitution, Alexander Hamilton, John Jay, and James Madison wrote 85 essays in the newspapers. The essays were part political theory, part practical politics, and part emotional persuasion.

Why important? *The Federalist Papers* are considered *the* handbook for understanding the U.S. Constitution.

299. TAFT-HARTLEY ACT

Truman and Eisenhower, 1945–1961

53. HAMILTON'S FINANCIAL PROGRAM

Truman and Eisenhower, 1945–1961

In the 1946 elections, Republicans gained a majority in the House and Senate for the first time since the 1920s. To keep another president from serving as long as Roosevelt did (he was elected four times, although he died shortly into his fourth term), Congress passed the 22nd Amendment (1951) limiting presidents to two terms in office.

Why important? This is an example of the constantly shifting balance of power between the executive and legislative branches of the federal government.

New Constitution and Government, 1787–1801

Secretary of the Treasury Alexander Hamilton created a program with these steps: 1) Pay off state debts. 2) Protect American business with high taxes (tariffs) on imported goods. 3) Create a government-run national bank to print money and to receive revenue from taxes. Thomas Jefferson opposed the bank idea, saying there was nothing about a government-run bank in the Constitution. As a "strict constructionist" Jefferson wanted no interpretations of the Constitution's intent. Hamilton, a "loose constructionist," said the elastic clause (the government can do what is "necessary and proper") allows for flexibility in the Constitution.

Why important? Hamilton's plan was enacted and had long-reaching effects **(#65)**, including Andrew Jackson's battle with the Second Bank of the United States **(#80)**. Arguments over interpretations of the Constitution continued throughout American history.

298. 22ND AMENDMENT

Truman and Eisenhower, 1945–1961

54. WHISKEY REBELLION

Truman and Eisenhower, 1945–1961

The Servicemen's Readjustment Act (G.I. Bill) of 1944 provided college tuition and low-interest home loans for veterans. These benefits still exist today for veterans.

Why important? The G.I. Bill made a college education and homeownership possible for millions of veterans after World War II.

New Constitution and Government, 1787–1801

Hamilton tested the effectiveness of the new government by placing a tax on whiskey in 1794. Corn farmers in Pennsylvania attacked tax collectors, and Washington sent U.S. soldiers to confront them. The farmers backed down.

Why important? The new government's swift reaction to this rebellion was a big contrast with the weaker response to Shays's Rebellion (**#48**) under the Articles of Confederation (**#47**).

---

297. G.I. BILL

Truman and Eisenhower, 1945–1961

Truman and Eisenhower, 1945–1961

After World War II ended, millions of soldiers returned home. Wage and price restrictions were lifted and inflation returned. Housing shortages appeared all over the country, and suburbs were built. Millions of babies were born over the next few years, in what is called the Baby Boom. The economy also boomed. Women left factories and returned to more traditional roles. African Americans fought for their civil rights.

Why important? The end of the war began profound social changes that continued over the next several decades.

New Constitution and Government, 1787–1801

55. WASHINGTON'S FAREWELL ADDRESS

After serving two terms as president, Washington chose not to run for a third. (The 22nd Amendment (1951) limited the presidency to two terms.) In his final message to the nation as president, Washington warned Americans not to get involved in European affairs, not to form permanent alliances, not to form political parties, and to avoid sectionalism—rivalries between different parts of the nation.

Why important? Washington's foreign policy advice was generally heeded by his successors until World War I, but political parties and sectionalism (**#72**) became important parts of the political landscape.

296. SOCIAL EFFECTS OF WORLD WAR II

Truman and Eisenhower, 1945–1961

56. KENTUCKY AND VIRGINIA RESOLUTIONS

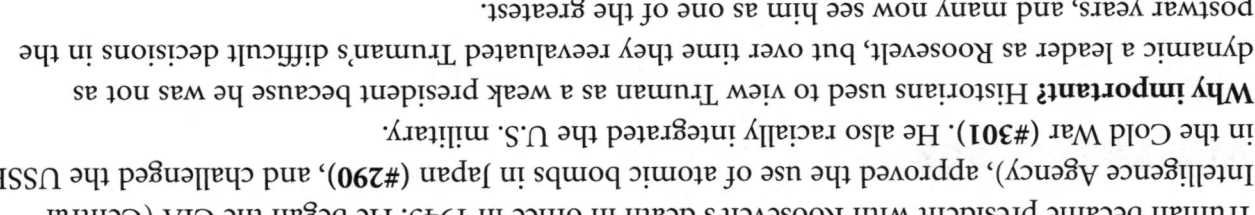

Truman and Eisenhower, 1945–1961

Truman became president with Roosevelt's death in office in 1945. He began the CIA (Central Intelligence Agency), approved the use of atomic bombs in Japan (**#290**), and challenged the USSR in the Cold War (**#301**). He also racially integrated the U.S. military.

Why important? Historians used to view Truman as a weak president because he was not as dynamic a leader as Roosevelt, but over time they reevaluated Truman's difficult decisions in the postwar years, and many now see him as one of the greatest.

New Constitution and Government, 1787–1801

Strained relations with France during John Adams's term (the XYZ Affair) led to congressional approval of the Alien and Sedition Acts, which made criticizing the president a crime. Opposition to these laws included the Kentucky and Virginia Resolutions of 1798. Claiming the doctrine of nullification (**#79**) both states threatened to leave the Union (secede) rather than enforce the Acts. The Acts were eventually overturned.

Why important? The idea that states could choose to leave the Union lasted until the Civil War.

295. HARRY TRUMAN

Truman and Eisenhower, 1945–1961

57. THE REVOLUTION OF 1800

In 1942 Roosevelt coined the term "United Nations" to refer to the Allies. By the end of the war, 50 nations agreed to expand into a world organization. The most important branch was the Security Council that dealt with military issues.

Why important? The UN was like the old League of Nations (**#231**) except that it had a military branch that could go to war to stop aggressive countries. Examples of such action include the Korean War (**#306**) and Persian Gulf War (**#345**).

Vice President Thomas Jefferson ran for president against John Adams in 1800. The Electoral College failed to select a winner, and the House of Representatives ultimately chose Jefferson after several votes. Jefferson was a member of the Democratic-Republican Party and opposed many of the policies of Adams's Federalist Party. Despite the election controversy, the transfer of power from one party to another was peaceful.

Why important? Later, the 12th Amendment to the Constitution required president and vice president to run on tickets from the same party (Jefferson had tied with the man who became his vice president, Aaron Burr). The peaceful transfer of power from one party to another showed the American experiment with a democratic republic was a success.

294. UNITED NATIONS

The Great Depression and World War II, 1929–1945

58. *AN ECONOMIC INTERPRETATION OF THE CONSTITUTION*

The Great Depression and World War II, 1929–1945

After Germany's defeat in World War II, Harry S. Truman, the new president, met with his Big Three counterparts, new British Prime Minister Clement Attlee and Soviet Premier Joseph Stalin, from July 17 to August 2, 1945. They agreed to demand unconditional surrender from Japan and hold trials for Nazi leaders in Nuremberg, Germany.

Why important? At Potsdam the Big Three finalized decisions made at the Yalta Conference (#292). In addition, Truman secretly told Attlee and Stalin of the successful test of the first atomic bomb in New Mexico.

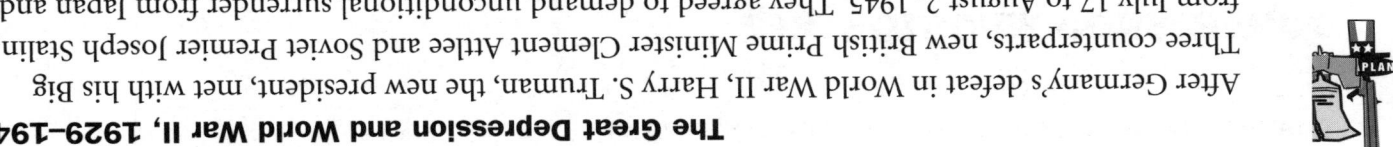

New Constitution and Government, 1787–1801

Charles Beard's 1913 book argued that the founding fathers were mainly influenced by their economic self-interest—not by their desire to create a government of, by, and for the people.

Why important? Beard's conclusions influenced historians and the greater American public for decades. More recent scholarship holds that the founders were more influenced by the political philosophies popular in the late 18th century than purely by economic gain.

---

293. POTSDAM CONFERENCE

The Great Depression and World War II, 1929–1945

59. LOUISIANA PURCHASE (1803)

The Great Depression and World War II, 1929–1945

In early 1945 the "Big Three," President Roosevelt, British Prime Minister Churchill, and Soviet Premier Stalin, met to discuss postwar plans in Europe and the partitioning of postwar Germany. Essentially, the USSR would be dominant in Eastern Europe while America and Britain would be dominant in Western Europe.

Why important? This redrawing of Europe's map set the stage for the Cold War (#301). During that era many people second-guessed Roosevelt's decision to "give" Eastern Europe to the USSR.

Jefferson Era, 1801–1824

Jefferson accepted the French dictator Napoleon's offer to sell his territory in North America, Louisiana, for around 15 million dollars. This area stretched roughly from the Mississippi River to the Rocky Mountains. Jefferson faced a quandary as a strict constructionist (**#53**), since the Constitution says nothing about the president buying land from foreign nations. However, the practical-minded Jefferson realized the deal was too good to pass up.

Why important? The Louisiana Purchase instantly doubled the size of the United States and gave it sole access to the vital Mississippi River.

292. YALTA CONFERENCE

The Great Depression and World War II, 1929–1945

The Great Depression and World War II, 1929–1945

As Allied forces entered Germany and neighboring countries to its east in the spring of 1945, they discovered the horrific extent to which the Nazis went to create a “pure” race. Approximately 10 million people were killed in death camps, most infamously at Auschwitz in Poland; 6 million were Jews.

Why important? After World War II the Allies held war crimes trials for the leaders of the Nazi movement, many of whom were convicted of “crimes against humanity.” The desire to prevent such brutality from ever happening again was a major factor in the creation of the United Nations (**#294**).

---

60. LEWIS AND CLARK EXPEDITION

Jefferson Era, 1801–1824

Jefferson Era, 1801–1824

Jefferson sent an Army expedition led by Meriwether Lewis and William Clark to explore the Louisiana Purchase. From 1804 to 1806 the group explored up the Missouri River and crossed to the Pacific Ocean in Oregon.

Why important? Lewis and Clark established friendly relations with Indians, found that there was no all-water route to the Pacific, and created maps for future settlement in the expansive area.

291. THE HOLOCAUST

The Great Depression and World War II, 1929–1945

On August 6, 1945 the United States dropped an atomic bomb on Hiroshima, Japan, destroying the city. Three days later Nagasaki, Japan was obliterated. Faced with threats of further annihilation, the Japanese empire unconditionally surrendered on August 15, 1945.

Why important? Debates over the use of atomic weapons in World War II continue. Proponents say it brought a quick end to the war, thus saving lives. Opponents say the use of atomic weapons to end the war was unnecessary and inhumane.

61. *MARBURY V. MADISON* (1803)

Jefferson Era, 1801–1824

This landmark Supreme Court case decided by Chief Justice John Marshall had to do with appointments to judgeships left over from the Adams administration ("midnight judges").

Why important? Marshall established the doctrine of judicial review, meaning the Supreme Court has the final say in all constitutional matters.

290. HIROSHIMA AND NAGASAKI

The Great Depression and World War II, 1929–1945

After the United States entered World War II, Albert Einstein wrote to President Roosevelt that an atomic super weapon was feasible and that America should build it before Nazi Germany did. In secret locations in Oak Ridge, Tennessee and Los Alamos, New Mexico scientists worked through the war to develop the atomic bomb. They successfully tested one in July 1945. Dr. Robert Oppenheimer led the project.

Why important? Not only did atomic weapons abruptly end World War II (**#290**), they also began the Atomic Age, in which unprecedented destruction was possible.

62. EMBARGO ACT (1807)

Jefferson Era, 1801–1824

England and France were at war. Both sides raided U.S. merchant ships and impressed sailors into service in their navies. The United States believed England was the chief culprit but rather than going to war over impressment, Jefferson imposed an embargo of imported goods to put economic pressure on England.

Why important? The plan was a disaster because the American economy was hurt much more than the English economy, and Jefferson repealed the Act.

289. MANHATTAN PROJECT

The Great Depression and World War II, 1929–1945

June 6, 1944 marked the invasion of Normandy (northern France) by Allied forces. Over 326,000 American, English, and Canadian soldiers were transported from England to Normandy. The commander of Operation Overlord (as it was called) was U.S. General Dwight Eisenhower (**#308**). "D-Day" was the name given to this first day of the major Allied offensive in Europe.

Why important? The invasion of Normandy was the turning point of the war in Europe in World War II.

63. WAR OF 1812 (1812–1815)

Jefferson Era, 1801–1824

By 1812, impressment and other issues pushed America and England into war. Many Americans wanted to take possession of British-held Canada. It was believed the British were stirring up anti-American sentiment among Indians on the frontier. Congressmen like John C. Calhoun and Henry Clay, the "War Hawks," clamored for war. Once war was declared, there was talk of secession (**#56, #111**) from New Englanders at the Hartford Convention. After a series of battles and few successes, America and England signed the Treaty of Ghent.

Why important? American victory at New Orleans (1815) just as the war ended created a surge of national pride. The Americans had fought England in two wars and won them both. The Federalist Party, which had opposed the war, faded in importance.

288. D-DAY

The Great Depression and World War II, 1929–1945

The Great Depression and World War II, 1929–1945

The U.S. strategy for victory in the Pacific in World War II was called "island-hopping." Instead of clearing every single island in the Pacific of Japan's troops, the United States attacked key islands and bypassed others, isolating Japan's forces.

Why important? Island-hopping was a quicker strategy in the push toward Japan than conventional means.

---

64. ERA OF GOOD FEELING

Jefferson Era, 1801–1824

Jefferson Era, 1801–1824

James Monroe was last of the Founding Fathers to serve as president, for two terms (1817–1825). His term saw a great era of optimism and national pride called the Era of Good Feeling.

Why important? In this era Americans came to believe they were members of one nation, rather than of individual states.

287. ISLAND-HOPPING

The Great Depression and World War II, 1929–1945

▼ 65. CLAY'S AMERICAN SYSTEM

U.S. and Filipino forces in the Philippines surrendered to the Japanese Army in 1942 and were forced on a brutal 63-mile march to a prison camp. While 70,000 captives began the march, only 54,000 arrived at the prison. Approximately 10,000 died on the way; the others escaped into the surrounding jungle.

Why important? The Bataan Death March was one of many examples of the brutality of World War II in the Pacific. This and Pearl Harbor (**#280**) were factors in the decision to drop two atomic bombs on Japan (**#290**).

Representative Henry Clay from Kentucky proposed a governmental plan similar to Hamilton's (#53) to promote the American economy. It included 1) a tax on imports (protective tariff), 2) a national bank, and 3) internal improvements (government-funded canals and roads). **Why important?** This system was adopted and is credited with fostering the basis of American economic success.

286. BATAAN DEATH MARCH

The Great Depression and World War II, 1929–1945

Seven months after Pearl Harbor, in June 1942, the American navy stopped a Japanese invasion of the Midway Islands (northwest of the Hawaiian Islands).

Why important? The Battle of Midway was the turning point of the war against Japan. From that point on, Japan was on the defensive and the United States and its allies pushed steadily toward the island nation.

Jefferson Era, 1801–1824

66. *MCCULLOCH V. MARYLAND* (1819)

Supreme Court Chief Justice John Marshall ruled the national bank created by Hamilton (**#53**) and re-chartered under the American System (**#65**) was constitutional because of the implied powers the Constitution grants the federal government.

Why important? This ruling solidified the power of the national government over the states and reinforced the Supreme Court's power to interpret the Constitution.

285. BATTLE OF MIDWAY

The Great Depression and World War II, 1929–1945

67. MISSOURI COMPROMISE

The federal government took strict control of the economy during World War II by freezing wages and prices. The Office of Price Administration (OPA) rationed sugar, beef, gasoline, shoes, and other items.

Why important? The OPA represents the most control the government ever exerted over the U.S. economy and shows the extent to which the government directed the war effort on the Home Front (#281).

In 1820 Kentucky Representative Henry Clay earned his reputation as the "Great Compromiser" by mediating a conflict in Congress over the admission of Missouri as a slave state. In the agreement approved by Congress, Missouri was allowed to be a slave state, Maine was admitted as a free state, and all the rest of the land in the Louisiana Purchase above Missouri's southern border outlawed slavery.

Why important? The Missouri Compromise touched off a debate over slavery that lasted until the Civil War and was the template for solving Congressional conflicts over slavery until 1850 (**#98**).

284. OFFICE OF PRICE ADMINISTRATION (1941)

The Great Depression and World War II, 1929–1945

During the Second World War, the U.S. government ordered all Japanese Americans to move to relocation camps in the northwestern states. Approximately 112,000 to 120,000 people were affected, 62% of whom were U.S. citizens. The Supreme Court ruled that the action was justified. **Why important?** This unjust treatment of Japanese Americans was due to the Japanese attack on Pearl Harbor (**#280**). No German or Italian Americans were sent to relocation camps. In the 1980s the federal government apologized to the families who were affected and provided financial compensation.

---

68. MONROE DOCTRINE

Jefferson Era, 1801–1824

Jefferson Era, 1801–1824

In 1823 President James Monroe declared that Europe was not to colonize any further in Latin America and not to interfere with countries in Latin America in the future. If they did, he said, the nations of Europe would have to answer to the United States.

Why important? The Monroe Doctrine was the most important foreign policy decision of the 19th century. It played a major part in the Spanish-American War (**#196**), the creation of the Panama Canal (**#207**), and in the 20th century, the Cuban Missile Crisis (**#324**).

283. JAPANESE INTERNMENT CAMPS

The Great Depression and World War II, 1929–1945

▼ 69. INDUSTRIAL INNOVATIONS, LATE 18TH, EARLY 19TH CENTURIES

In World War II, women worked in factories building planes, tanks, jeeps, and ships because millions of men had left their jobs to join the military. "Rosie the Riveter" appeared on posters and in films as a recruiting figure and a symbol of these women's efforts. After the war, soldiers returned to their jobs and women to their homes.

Why important? Not only did women support the war effort in this way, but some claim they also paved the way for women who wished to enter male-dominated professions (#329, #348).

Jefferson Era, 1801–1824

Eli Whitney produced the cotton gin (1793) and interchangeable parts. Samuel Slater introduced the cotton-thread factory system in 1791, which led to the Lowell factory system in Massachusetts during the 1830s. The McCormick Reaper and John Deere's steel plow increased agricultural productivity.

Why important? The cotton gin created a boom in the demand for cotton and slaves; the use of interchangeable parts greatly shortened production time and led to the modern assembly line. The Lowell system became the model for other factories throughout the 19th century. The steel plow turned what had been the "Great American Desert" into the Great Plains (**#87**).

---

282. ROSIE THE RIVETER

The Great Depression and World War II, 1929–1945

The Great Depression and World War II, 1929–1945

During World War II the name "Home Front" referred to the efforts of men, women, and children living in the United States to support the military. People planted "victory gardens" in their backyards; children collected metal in scrap drives to supply material for tanks, airplanes, and ships; and movies and radio programs reflected patriotic themes.

Why important? In World War II, Americans were strongly united behind the war effort and eager to do their part.

Jefferson Era, 1801–1824

70. TRANSPORTATION IMPROVEMENTS, EARLY 19TH CENTURY

Jefferson Era, 1801–1824

The world's first steamboat, the *Clermont*, built by Robert Fulton, sailed the Hudson River in 1807. A federally funded national road, the Cumberland Road, was built from Maryland to Illinois from 1811 to the 1850s. The Erie Canal in New York (1825) provided a big boost to that region's economy and triggered other canal projects. By the 1830s, railroad lines connected cities with reliable transportation.

Why important? Fast and efficient transportation meant lower prices for goods and an expanding national economy.

---

281. HOME FRONT

The Great Depression and World War II, 1929–1945

The Great Depression and World War II, 1929–1945

On December 7, 1941, "a date that will live in infamy" according to Roosevelt, the Japanese attacked U.S. military bases in Hawaii, most importantly ships anchored in Pearl Harbor. Over 2000 Americans were killed and the U.S. Pacific Fleet was badly crippled.

Why important? This surprise attack led to a declaration of war on Japan the next day, and the United States officially entered World War II.

71. PANIC OF 1819

Jefferson Era, 1801–1824

Jefferson Era, 1801–1824

The economy took a sharp downturn in the Monroe administration with the Panic of 1819. A chief cause was land speculation. Too many people borrowed money from banks to buy land from the government, usually in the West. When the land didn't sell, people defaulted on loans, banks closed, and unemployment increased sharply.

Why important? The Panic of 1819 was the first big economic downturn since the ratification of the Constitution and put a damper on the nationalist spirit of the Era of Good Feeling (**#64**).

280. PEARL HARBOR

The Great Depression and World War II, 1929–1945

Jefferson Era, 1801–1824

72. SECTIONALISM

The Great Depression and World War II, 1929–1945

In the summer of 1941, President Roosevelt and British Prime Minister Winston Churchill met on a warship in the Atlantic Ocean to discuss fighting the German navy in the Atlantic and the two countries' war aims. A month earlier, the United States had begun attacking all German ships in the Atlantic on sight.

Why important? Months before America officially entered World War II it was fighting Germany in the Atlantic Ocean.

Jefferson Era, 1801–1824

After the Era of Good Feeling (**#64**) the three main regions of the nation—North, West, and South—increasingly saw themselves as distinct. The North was the most industrialized with many railroads and factories. The South had slaves, wealthy planters, and small farmers. The West saw many settlers on the move. (In the early 19th century, Tennessee to the Mississippi River was "the West.")

Why important? Factions arose in Congress over issues that favored one region but hurt another. Suspicions about people in "other" parts of the country fed into the growing conflicts that became the Civil War.

---

279. ATLANTIC CHARTER

The Great Depression and World War II, 1929–1945

Jackson Era, 1824–1844

73. CORRUPT BARGAIN

The Great Depression and World War II, 1929–1945

Franklin Roosevelt wanted to help England against Germany in World War II, but the United States was officially neutral before the Japanese attack on Pearl Harbor (December 1941) (**#280**). In 1939, he convinced Congress to amend the Neutrality Act of 1937 (**#276**) to allow England to buy U.S. weapons. In 1940, Roosevelt traded 50 U.S. warships to England in exchange for naval bases in the Caribbean (to protect southern U.S. ports). The last step before Pearl Harbor was the Lend-Lease Act, which basically gave weapons to England, the USSR, and China to fight Germany and Japan.

Why important? These policies were surreptitious ways around the government's neutral stance before the United States joined the war.

In 1824, Andrew Jackson, Henry Clay, and John Quincy Adams ran for president. The disputed election results were settled by the House of Representatives, where Clay gave his support—and therefore the election—to Adams. Adams then named Clay his secretary of state. Jackson complained that his two rivals had made a "corrupt bargain."

Why important? Jackson immediately began campaigning for the 1828 election, when he defeated John Quincy Adams.

▲ 278. LEND-LEASE ACT (1941)

The Great Depression and World War II, 1929–1945

74. AGE OF THE COMMON MAN

World War II started in Europe in 1939. The United States was at heart largely on the Allies' side (primarily England and France at the time), but officially the nation was neutral. Americans favoring non-involvement formed the America First Committee. Its most famous spokesman was the 1920s aviator Charles Lindbergh (**#239**) who warned against participating in another "European" world war.

Why important? Before the Japanese bombed Pearl Harbor in 1941 (**#280**), the America First Committee was widely popular, but it quickly disappeared after the United States entered World War II.

Jackson Era, 1824–1844

Andrew Jackson, hero of the Battle of New Orleans, self-made man, and wealthy plantation owner from Tennessee, embodied what many Americans hoped to be. Nearly all white males were eligible to vote in 1828 and they overwhelmingly voted for "Old Hickory." Jackson was the first president from the Democratic Party and from the West.

Why important? With this new expression of democracy came reform movements from every corner, advocating causes such as women's rights, abolition, and humane treatment of prisoners and the mentally ill (#77).

---

277. AMERICA FIRST COMMITTEE

The Great Depression and World War II, 1929–1945

The Great Depression and World War II, 1929–1945

Traditionally historians have argued that the United States was isolationist in the 1920s and '30s. The strongest evidence in support of that claim is that the United States didn't join the League of Nations, and it was neutral in the German-backed Spanish Civil War (the Neutrality Act of 1937 forbade participation in foreign conflicts and armament sales to nations at war). However, counterexamples include the Washington Conference and Kellogg-Briand Pact (**#245**). Also, in the 1930s America recognized the communist government of the Soviet Union, and the Good Neighbor Policy (**#275**) was established with Latin American nations.

Why important? Most of the American people probably *did* support isolationism, but the government stayed involved in international affairs.

75. SECOND GREAT AWAKENING

Jackson Era, 1824–1844

Jackson Era, 1824–1844

A religious revival began in the early 19th century and grew through the Jackson era.

Why important? It sparked several major developments in religion and reform movements. The Mormons, or Church of Latter Day Saints, were founded by Joseph Smith and Brigham Young. After facing much persecution in the Northeast and Midwest, the Mormons migrated to Utah in the 1830s. Utopian communities, often based on religious foundations, arose around the nation. Brook Farm in Massachusetts, New Harmony in Indiana, and the Oneida Community in New York were attempts to create perfect societies isolated from the rest of the world. All failed.

▲ 276. ISOLATIONISM

The Great Depression and World War II, 1929–1945

The Great Depression and World War II, 1929–1945

President Franklin D. Roosevelt sought to improve relations with Latin America by promising to never interfere with the internal politics of the nations there. He also cancelled the Platt Amendment (**#204**), which called for U.S. involvement in Cuban affairs.

Why important? FDR hoped better relations with the nearby Latin American nations would help unite this part of the world against Germany's aggressive foreign policy. The Good Neighbor Policy did keep the United States and Latin America united against the fascist countries in the World War II era.

▼ 76. ART AND LITERATURE OF THE EARLY 19TH CENTURY

Jackson Era, 1824–1844

Jackson Era, 1824–1844

The Hudson River school was a popular artistic style that promoted national pride with beautiful paintings of American nature. Transcendentalism was a philosophy that attracted writers Ralph Waldo Emerson and Henry David Thoreau. The latter wrote *Walden* and the essay "On Civil Disobedience." Transcendentalists believed in searching for God in nature and in returning to a simpler lifestyle. Other important writers were Washington Irving, James Fennimore Cooper, and Nathaniel Hawthorne.

Why important? An American style of literature developed and became respected here and in Europe in this era.

---

275. GOOD NEIGHBOR POLICY (1933–1945)

The Great Depression and World War II, 1929–1945

The Great Depression and World War II, 1929–1945

Some historians say the New Deal was a revolution that changed the purpose and practices of the national government. Others say the New Deal was just a continuance of the Progressive programs that had already begun increasing the size and power of the federal government.

Why important? This debate demonstrates that historians never settle on, once and for all, *the* interpretation of the past.

77. JACKSON ERA REFORM MOVEMENTS

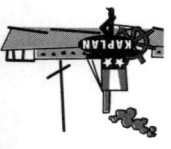

The temperance movement opposed alcohol consumption. Dorothea Dix pushed for the rights of the mentally ill, who were often put in jails. The focus of prisons switched to reform rather than solely punishment. Elizabeth Cady Stanton and Lucretia Mott promoted equal rights for women, leading the Seneca Falls Convention in New York in 1848. William Lloyd Garrison published the abolitionist (antislavery) newspaper, *The Liberator.*

Why important? The temperance movement reached its political goal with the 18th Amendment outlawing alcoholic beverages in 1919. Dix's efforts led to the building of mental hospitals. Women received the right to vote from the 19th Amendment in 1920. The abolition movement was a long-term cause of the Civil War.

274. ANALYSIS OF THE NEW DEAL

The Great Depression and World War II, 1929–1945

The Great Depression and World War II, 1929–1945

During the Great Depression, a drought hit the Great Plains, causing even more poverty than already existed. Thousands of families migrated out of the "Dust Bowl" states such as Oklahoma between 1930 and 1941. Most headed to California looking for work as farm laborers (as depicted in John Steinbeck's 1939 novel, *The Grapes of Wrath*).

Why important? As if the Depression weren't enough, Dust Bowl conditions struck another damaging blow to many American farmers in this era.

78. TRAIL OF TEARS

Jackson Era, 1824–1844

Jackson Era, 1824–1844

Like most voters of the time, Jackson believed white settlers and Indians should not live close to each other. In 1830 he signed the Indian Removal Act. Thousands of Cherokees in the southeast were forced to move to Oklahoma along what is known as the "Trail of Tears." Supreme Court Chief Justice John Marshall ruled in *Worcester v. Georgia* that the Indians should stay on their original land. Jackson openly defied the ruling.

Why important? Jackson's decision revealed a truth about the democratic Age of the Common Man: it referred only to white men.

273. DUST BOWL

The Great Depression and World War II, 1929–1945

79. NULLIFICATION CRISIS (1832)

The 20th Amendment moved the date of the presidential inauguration from March 4 up to January 20. It was first applied in 1937.

Why important? Newly elected presidents no longer had to wait five months to take office. With improved transportation and communication since the late 19th century, it no longer made sense for a new president to wait so long to take office.

South Carolina refused to pay the federal tariff (import taxes), calling it the "Tariff of Abominations." Its politicians cited the nullification theory **(#56),** claiming that states could ignore federal laws they thought were wrong, and threatened to secede. Jackson, usually a states-rights supporter, sided against South Carolina and for preserving the Union. In Congress Daniel Webster and Robert Hayne famously debated the issue. When Henry Clay forged the lower Compromise Tariff of 1833 and when Jackson threatened to invade South Carolina, the state backed down. **Why important?** The nullification doctrine was reused in the Civil War (**#111**).

272. 20th AMENDMENT

The Great Depression and World War II, 1929–1945

Until the New Deal the U.S. government set no minimum that a company had to pay a worker. Starting in 1938, the first minimum wage was set at 25 cents per hour.

Why important? This was the last major New Deal program, and it still exists today.

Jackson Era, 1824–1844

80. SECOND BANK OF THE UNITED STATES

Jackson Era, 1824–1844

Jackson hated the Second Bank of the United States (**#53, #65**), claiming it was an unconstitutional use of the federal government's power and that it enriched the wealthy at the expense of the masses. Jackson dissolved the bank and deposited its money into smaller banks around the country, called "pet banks" by his enemies. Then he issued the Specie Circular to curb inflation. This required all purchases of federal land (mostly in the West) to be made in gold or silver.

Why important? Killing the bank and issuing the Specie Circular led to an economic depression, the Panic of 1837.

271. MINIMUM WAGE

The Great Depression and World War II, 1929–1945

Jackson Era, 1824–1844

81. THE LOG CABIN CAMPAIGN OF 1840

The Great Depression and World War II, 1929–1945

John L. Lewis headed the Congress of Industrial Organizations (CIO), formed in 1935 and a rival to the more established American Federation of Labor (AFL) (**#178**). Unlike the AFL, the CIO organized *unskilled* automotive, steel, and textile workers.

Why important? After years of competing against each other, the AFL and CIO united in the 1950s to form the nation's most powerful labor union.

Jackson Era, 1824–1844

Jackson served two terms in office. Voters elected his friend, Martin Van Buren, in 1836. In 1840, Van Buren ran for reelection against Whig candidate and War of 1812 hero, "Old Tippecanoe" William Henry Harrison. The Whig Party was formed during Jackson's administration by people who opposed the policies of "King Andrew the First." Harrison was portrayed as a common man who, like Jackson, came from humble origins. The first famous campaign slogan, "Tippecanoe and Tyler too!" was used (John Tyler was running for vice president). The Panic of 1837 (**#80**) ruined Van Buren's chances for reelection.

Why important? The 1840 campaign was the most colorful of the 19th century and saw the highest percentage of voter turnout in the 19th century.

270. CIO

The Great Depression and World War II, 1929–1945

The Great Depression and World War II, 1929–1945

In 1935, the U.S. Congress approved the Wagner Act. This Act created the National Labor Relations Board, a government committee that could intervene in disputes between labor and management if necessary. It guaranteed the rights of unions to represent workers.

Why important? Laborers struggled for decades to get unions legalized and protected by the national government. Following federal recognition, unions became powerful organizations in American politics.

82. MANIFEST DESTINY

Westward Expansion, 1820s–1850s

Westward Expansion, 1820s–1850s

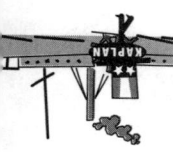

In the 1840s many Americans believed it was the nation's "manifest destiny" to extend its borders from the Atlantic to the Pacific.

Why important? This belief spurred migration to the West beyond the Mississippi River all the way to the Pacific Ocean and was a major cause of the Mexican War (**#85**).

▲ 269. WAGNER ACT

The Great Depression and World War II, 1929–1945

The Great Depression and World War II, 1929–1945

The Social Security Act (1935) was a Second New Deal (**#266**) federal program. It provided (and continues to provide) a monthly income to retired Americans. It also funded unemployment compensation as a safety net for people who lost their jobs and couldn't find work.

Why important? Social Security is the most famous and extensive New Deal program. Over time, the number of people who qualified for Social Security benefits expanded greatly, as did the program's cost.

83. TEXAS

Westward Expansion, 1820s–1850s

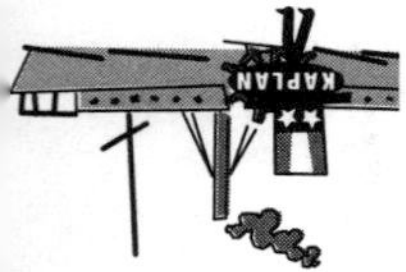

American settlers began moving into Texas in the 1820s and lived under Mexican laws. By the 1830s so many had poured in that their presence concerned the Mexican government. In 1836, Sam Houston declared an independent Republic of Texas, so Mexican leader Antonio Lopez de Santa Anna attacked Americans at the Alamo in San Antonio. Santa Anna was later defeated by Houston and agreed to recognize Texan independence. In 1845 the United States added Texas to the Union as a slave state.

Why important? Conflict over Texas was a cause of the Mexican War (**#85**) but its addition to the Union greatly increased the size of the nation.

268. SOCIAL SECURITY ACT

The Great Depression and World War II, 1929–1945

The Works Progress Administration (WPA) was a Second New Deal (**#266**) program that spent billions of dollars creating jobs for the unemployed building roads, bridges, and schools, as well as raking leaves, acting in plays, and binding books.

Why important? The WPA was the biggest of the make-work New Deal programs that sought to end the Depression by creating jobs and thus getting money back into the economy. Critics called the make-work programs, like leaf-raking, "boondoggles."

84. "FIFTY-FOUR FORTY OR FIGHT!"

Westward Expansion, 1820s–1850s

This was the slogan of the Democrats when James K. Polk ran for president in 1844. It referred to a boundary dispute with England over the northern border of the Oregon territory. Americans wanted Oregon to extend up to the lowest border of Russian-held Alaska, and England wanted to extend Canada down to the southern border of modern-day Washington State.

Why important? Polk won the election with this slogan but later the United States and England negotiated a border at 49 degrees north latitude, the current northern boundary of Washington State.

267. WPA

The Great Depression and World War II, 1929–1945

The Second New Deal was a later phase of the original New Deal and was an answer to critics who said the New Deal didn't go far enough. Second New Deal programs were proposed and implemented in 1935 (two years after the "first" New Deal), and most were more extensive. Social Security (**#268**), the Wagner Act (**#269**), and the WPA (**#267**) were three Second New Deal programs.

Why important? Historians debate whether the Second New Deal was a radical departure from the first New Deal or a natural political progression. Programs such as Social Security still exist.

---

85. MEXICAN WAR

Westward Expansion, 1820s–1850s

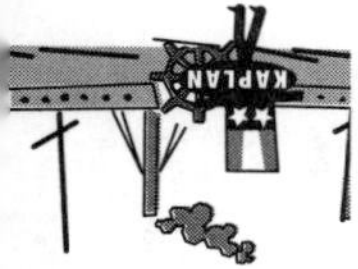

Tensions rose between Mexico and America over America's annexation of Texas in 1845 (**#83**). In 1846 a U.S. Army patrol to the Mexican border claimed it was attacked and cries for war began in Congress. War was declared and the American army captured the capital and defeated the Mexicans. In the Treaty of Guadalupe Hidalgo (1848), Mexico recognized the current Texas border and sold California, Utah, Nevada, and parts of New Mexico, Arizona, Wyoming, and Colorado to the United States: the Mexican Cession.

Why important? Manifest Destiny (**#82**) was achieved, relations between the United States and Mexico remained sour, and future Civil War generals received their combat training.

266. SECOND NEW DEAL

The Great Depression and World War II, 1929–1945

86. GADSDEN PURCHASE

Some politicians, like Franklin D. Roosevelt's 1936 presidential opponent Alf Landon, opposed the New Deal for going too far toward socialism. Others, like Dr. Francis Townsend, argued the New Deal didn't go far enough. Townsend, for example, wanted the government to pay elderly people a monthly salary.

Why important? FDR crushed Landon in 1936, proving the New Deal was popular. FDR countered his more liberal opponents by modifying some of their ideas and making them his own. The best example is Social Security, which provides income for the retired (#268).

The southern border of present-day New Mexico and Arizona was established with this land purchase from Mexico for a railroad route (1853).

Why important? Some believe the high price America paid for this land ($10 million) was a form of apology for the outcome of the Mexican War.

265. NEW DEAL OPPOSITION

The Great Depression and World War II, 1929–1945

The Supreme Court struck down the AAA (**#260**) and the NRA (**#259**) as unconstitutional. Franklin D. Roosevelt criticized the court, calling the justices "nine old men." He proposed adding extra (pro-FDR) members to the Supreme Court, but his idea went nowhere due to popular rejection.

Why important? FDR's "court packing" proposal was his only major political miscalculation as president. However, many of the older members of the Court retired not long after this and FDR replaced them with New Deal-friendly judges.

87. ROUTES WEST

Westward Expansion, 1820s–1850s

Westward Expansion, 1820s–1850s

From the 1820s to the end of the 1850s, three primary routes were taken by Americans migrating from East to West. 1) The wagon train consisted of settlers who traveled in groups of wagons across the "Great American Desert," later called the Great Plains (**#69**). This was the most popular method. A popular "jumping-off point" was Independence, Missouri. 2) People with more money sometimes took a clipper ship (**#89**) under South America and up to California. 3) On the fastest and most expensive route, the Isthmus Crossing, settlers sailed to present-day Panama, crossed the isthmus on foot, and picked up a ship on the Pacific side to California.

Why important? Hundreds of thousands of people moved West during this era in the biggest migration in American history.

264. COURT PACKING

The Great Depression and World War II, 1929–1945

Westward Expansion, 1820s–1850s

88. FORTY-NINERS

The Great Depression and World War II, 1929–1945

The Tennessee Valley Authority (TVA) was a New Deal program that built dams in the Tennessee River valley to provide hydroelectric power to the region. This part of the country was terribly poor until the TVA provided electricity. **Why important?** The TVA still exists today and is still a government-run electricity provider. Over the next decades several similar projects were created all over the country.

Westward Expansion, 1820s–1850s

Gold was found near Sacramento, California in 1848 and by the next year everybody in the nation had heard about it. This began a gold rush to California; those who traveled there looking for fortune were called "Forty-Niners." Other gold rushes occurred in Colorado and Nevada in the 1850s, the Dakotas in the 1870s, and Alaska in the 1890s.

Why important? The gold fever was the greatest reason why record-setting numbers of people headed West during this era.

263. TVA

The Great Depression and World War II, 1929–1945

The Great Depression and World War II, 1929–1945

The Civilian Conservation Corps (CCC) was a New Deal relief program that sent unemployed young men from cities into the countryside around the nation to perform conservation work in parks and woods.

Why important? The CCC is an example of the "try anything" attitude of the New Deal administrators. Many parks and wooded areas all over the nation were improved.

89. INDUSTRIAL TECHNOLOGY OF THE MID-19TH CENTURY

Westward Expansion, 1820s–1850s

Westward Expansion, 1820s–1850s

Elias Howe invented the sewing machine. Samuel F.B. Morse developed the telegraph and the communication language for it. America's development of clipper ships meant the United States had the fastest sailing vessels of the era. However, by the mid-1850s steamboats took their place. In 1854 U.S. Navy Commodore Matthew C. Perry steamed to Japan and forced the reluctant nation into a trading agreement.

Why important? Howe's invention revolutionized the clothing industry, increasing production and lowering prices dramatically. With the telegraph, fast communication over long distances was possible. Clipper ships and ocean-going steamboats proved America was a major force in sea trade. Perry's "opening" of Japan prodded that nation into developing a modern economy and military force.

262. CCC

The Great Depression and World War II, 1929–1945

90. ANTEBELLUM PERIOD

The Federal Deposit Insurance Corporation was created in the New Deal to protect people's money in banks. The government required banks that participated in the program to contribute money to an insurance fund to cover deposits put in banks that failed.

Why important? The FDIC, one of the alphabet agencies (#258), was one of the reform programs of the New Deal and is a vital part of the banking industry today.

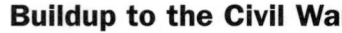

Buildup to the Civil War

This was the era between the War of 1812 and the Civil War. (Antebellum is Latin for "before the war.") After James K. Polk served his term, the presidents of this era were generally weak.

Why important? The South grew in economic and political power. Political and social arguments over slavery increased, culminating in war.

261. FDIC

The Great Depression and World War II, 1929–1945

The Agricultural Adjustment Administration (AAA) was a New Deal recovery program that was a kind of NRA (**#259**) for farmers. It paid farmers not to plant crops (farm subsidies) in order to reduce production, thereby increasing prices.

Why important? Like the NRA, the AAA was struck down by the Supreme Court but returned later in a different form. The U.S. government still provides farm subsidies and works to coordinate the amount of agricultural produce.

▼ 91. "KING COTTON"

The most important crop to the South by far in the antebellum period (**#90**) was cotton. It was America's biggest export. Because cotton farming was so labor-intensive, slavery became even more essential to the Southern economy.

Why important? Cotton was the greatest reason for the South's increasing economic and political power before the Civil War.

260. AAA

The Great Depression and World War II, 1929–1945

Buildup to the Civil War

92. PECULIAR INSTITUTION

The Great Depression and World War II, 1929–1945

The National Recovery Administration (NRA) was a New Deal program that was designed to work with business and labor workers to establish fair wages and reasonable profits. It also permitted unions and collective bargaining (each worker doesn't have to negotiate his pay scale; instead, unions and management set pay rates for groups of workers).

Why important? The Supreme Court ruled the NRA and the AAA (**#260**) were unconstitutional. This led to the "court packing" controversy (**#264**).

Southerners who defended slavery used this term to describe it ("peculiar" meant "different," not "strange"). They argued that Northerners who opposed slavery weren't in a position to truly understand it, so Northerners shouldn't criticize it. According to this concept, only those who practiced or supported slavery understood it well enough to have an opinion about it.

Why important? As opposition to slavery grew in the antebellum period, so did the numbers of ways its supporters tried to defend it—or at least, change the argument.

259. NRA

The Great Depression and World War II, 1929–1945

The Great Depression and World War II, 1929–1945

New Deal legislation included the creation of many new government agencies designed to end the Great Depression. Most were known by their initials, like the TVA (**#263**), WPA (**#267**), CCC (**#262**), AAA (**#260**), and NRA (**#259**). Franklin Roosevelt's top advisors, many of whom created these agencies, were called the "Brain Trust" (**#254**).

Why important? The TVA, the FDIC (**#261**), and the FHA (Federal Housing Administration) are just three of many New Deal agencies still around.

Buildup to the Civil War

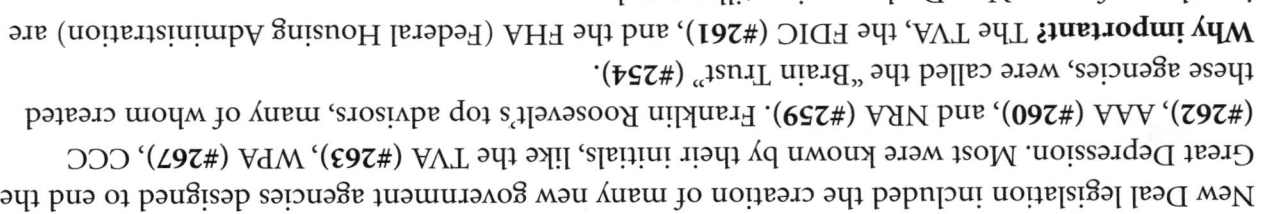

93. NAT TURNER SLAVE REVOLT

This most famous of the relatively few slave revolts in the South occurred in 1831 in Virginia, led by slave Nat Turner.

Why important? The largest of all slave revolts, it failed but led to increased slave patrols, suspicions, and racial tension in the South.

258. ALPHABET AGENCIES

The Great Depression and World War II, 1929–1945

94. SOCIAL HIERARCHY IN THE ANTEBELLUM SOUTH

The Great Depression and World War II, 1929–1945

Throughout his presidency, Franklin D. Roosevelt spoke on the radio to the American people in an informal one-to-one style called "fireside chats."

Why important? By using the relatively new mass medium of radio, FDR created a bond of trust with the nation. Presidents ever since have worked to develop good media skills to foster a connection with the public.

Buildup to the Civil War

Most Southerners did not own slaves, but the pinnacle of Southern society consisted of the planter class—people who owned 60 or more slaves and sizeable plantations. Next were professionals—doctors and merchants, for example, some of whom owned slaves. Next came middle-class (yeoman) farmers who owned less land and fewer slaves. The poor farmers at the bottom of white society still were at a level higher than slaves.

Why important? Slavery defined the social order of the South.

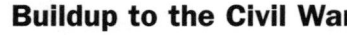

257. FIRESIDE CHATS

The Great Depression and World War II, 1929–1945

95. SOUTHERN DEFENSE OF SLAVERY

The Great Depression and World War II, 1929–1945

Despite the 18th Amendment prohibiting the consumption of alcohol (#220), in the 1920s and early 1930s the illegal use of alcohol was rampant. The 21st Amendment repealed the 18th Amendment in 1933. Immediately the federal and many state budgets benefited from the revenue generated by taxes on liquor.

Why important? The Progressive-era attempt to stop alcohol consumption failed. The 18th Amendment is the only one to have been repealed.

As the number of slaves increased (to almost 4 million by 1860) so did pressure from abolitionists. In response, supporters of slavery developed several defenses of the "peculiar institution" (**#92**), including the following: slavery is in the Bible; slave owners provide free food, clothing, medical care, and shelter; slave owners Christianize and civilize slaves.

Why important? Supporters of slavery refused to be silent while their way of life was attacked, escalating anger and rhetoric between North and South.

256. 21ST AMENDMENT

Buildup to the Civil War

96. FREDERICK DOUGLASS

The Great Depression and World War II, 1929–1945

A record amount of legislation was sped through Congress in President Franklin D. Roosevelt's first hundred days, like the NRA (**#259**), AAA (**#260**), and TVA (**#263**). Roosevelt also called for a one-day "bank holiday" in this period, closing all banks to stop the panicked withdrawals. **Why important?** Ever since FDR, presidents have traditionally had a "honeymoon" of 100 days with the press and Congress. The bank holiday worked, stopping the nationwide runs on the banks.

This abolition (#77) leader was born into slavery, and so was particularly able to address its evils. **Why important?** Douglass was famous in the North because he was an eloquent speaker and the publisher of an abolitionist paper, *The North Star*.

---

255. HUNDRED DAYS

The Great Depression and World War II, 1929–1945

The Great Depression and World War II, 1929–1945

This was the nickname of Franklin D. Roosevelt's group of advisors who developed New Deal programs. ("Trust" is an older term meaning "corporation.")

Why important? The main figures of Roosevelt's brain trust were the members of his legal counsel and academics such as Raymond Moley, Rexford Tugwell, and Adolf Berle. In addition to his brain trust, members of Roosevelt's cabinet including Harry Hopkins, Harold Ickes, and Frances Perkins also created New Deal programs. Perkins was the first woman to be a member of a president's cabinet.

---

97. UNDERGROUND RAILROAD

Buildup to the Civil War

Buildup to the Civil War

Escaped slaves followed secret routes from South to North, often into Canada. Harriet Tubman and Sojourner Truth became famous for leading people out of slavery.

Why important? In both North and South, abolitionist sympathizers risked fines and jail when they allowed escaped slaves to hide on their property.

254. BRAIN TRUST

The Great Depression and World War II, 1929–1945

New Deal programs fell into three categories: 1) Relief (sending money to people out of work), 2) Recovery (pulling the nation out of the Great Depression), and 3) Reform (insuring that similar economic disasters didn't happen again). One relief program was welfare, which was money sent from the government to the jobless. The idea was to provide assistance to desperate people during the Depression. The NRA was a recovery program (**#259**), and the FDIC (**#261**) was a reform program.

Why important? Until the New Deal, the national government did not provide economic help to individuals in need and did little to pull the economy out of slumps. This depression was so severe, however, that President Roosevelt believed extraordinary action had to be taken.

98. COMPROMISE OF 1850

Henry Clay's (**#67**) last compromise included several provisions. 1) California was admitted to the Union as a free state. 2) The slave trade became illegal in Washington, DC but slavery was still legal there. 3) The Fugitive Slave Law made it easier for slave owners to recapture escaped slaves. **Why important?** This final compromise between defenders and opponents of slavery held off the Civil War for 10 years.

253. RELIEF, RECOVERY, REFORM

The Great Depression and World War II, 1929–1945

Buildup to the Civil War

99. *UNCLE TOM'S CABIN*

The Great Depression and World War II, 1929–1945

Eleanor Roosevelt was Franklin D. Roosevelt's wife and his number-one spokesperson. She traveled around America promoting New Deal programs and later the war effort. After her husband's death she was named U.S. Ambassador to the United Nations.

Why important? Eleanor Roosevelt was the first modern First Lady, one who didn't live quietly in the shadow of her husband.

Harriet Beecher Stowe's novel depicted the mistreatment of slaves on a plantation. It became the most-read novel of its time, and it angered many on both sides of the slavery question. Opponents of slavery saw it as a true depiction of life in the South, but those who defended slavery said it unfairly painted all slave owners as evil.

Why important? Lincoln later called Stowe "the little lady who made this big war."

252. ELEANOR ROOSEVELT

The Great Depression and World War II, 1929–1945

The Great Depression and World War II, 1929–1945

This was President Franklin D. Roosevelt's name for his plan to pull America out of the Great Depression with massive government aid. The New Deal included programs like welfare, Social Security (**#268**), and unemployment compensation, as well as road and building construction projects all over the nation.

Why important? The New Deal greatly increased the power of government over the economy and in people's everyday lives. The size and cost of the national government also increased enormously.

100. POPULAR SOVEREIGNTY

Buildup to the Civil War

Buildup to the Civil War

This was a political attempt in the 1850s to ease tensions over the status of slavery in new territories. Under Popular Sovereignty, when a region gained enough people to officially form a territory the voters chose whether or not to allow slavery.

Why important? See the Kansas-Nebraska Act (**#101**).

▲ 251. NEW DEAL

The Great Depression and World War II, 1929–1945

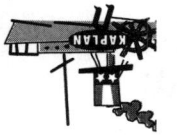

The Great Depression and World War II, 1929–1945

Franklin Delano Roosevelt was president from 1933 to 1945. He was the only president elected for four terms (or even three terms). He is known for saying, "The only thing we have to fear is fear itself." Despite his physical handicap (paralyzed legs) he exuded optimism through the Great Depression and World War II.

Why important? FDR greatly expanded the power of the president and the role of government in people's lives. He provided outstanding leadership during two of this country's greatest crises. He also forged a coalition of Democrats including minorities, labor workers, and the poor, which remained unchallenged until the 1980s.

101. KANSAS-NEBRASKA ACT

Buildup to the Civil War

Congress passed this law in 1854. It let voters in these two new territories decide for themselves whether slavery would be allowed there (**#100**). Both Kansas and Nebraska were above the Missouri Compromise line (**#67**).

Why important? Despite its intentions, the Kansas-Nebraska Act increased antagonism between North and South and led to violence in Kansas and in Congress (**#103**).

---

250. FRANKLIN D. ROOSEVELT

The Great Depression and World War II, 1929–1945

102. STEPHEN A. DOUGLAS

The Great Depression and World War II, 1929–1945

In 1932, at the height of the Depression, hundreds of unemployed World War I veterans met in Washington, DC to ask the government for an advance on a bonus that been promised to them, which wasn't due until 1945. President Hoover sent the army to run them out of town without the bonus.

Why important? This confrontational approach against U.S. veterans made Hoover appear heartless, and he lost support in his 1932 election campaign against Democrat Franklin Roosevelt.

This Illinois senator developed the concept of Popular Sovereignty (**#100**) and the Kansas-Nebraska Act (**#101**). His nickname was "The Little Giant" for his small stature and big speaking voice. He famously defeated Abraham Lincoln in the race for the Illinois senate in 1858 (**#108**).

Why important? Douglas was one of the Senate's most influential leaders in the 1850s, but his connection with the controversial Kansas-Nebraska Act (**#101**) and a split within his party hurt him in the presidential election of 1860, which went to Lincoln (**#110**).

249. BONUS MARCH

103. “BLEEDING KANSAS” AND BROOKS-SUMNER ATTACK

The Great Depression and World War II, 1929–1945

During the economic boom of the late ’20s, Republican Herbert Hoover was elected president. The Great Depression (**#246**) struck 7 months into his presidency. Hoover attempted to ease the effects of the Crash of ’29 with the Reconstruction Finance Corporation, a government agency that loaned money to major businesses like railroads and banks, but the Depression was far deeper than he realized.

Why important? The RFC was the first government program designed to end an economic slump, but for decades afterward, Hoover was blamed for the Great Depression. Historians have since given him more credit for attempting to end it.

Buildup to the Civil War

Violence erupted in Kansas when pro-and antislavery settlers attacked each other between 1854 and 1856. Approximately 200 people were killed throughout the territory. In Washington, DC, pro-slavery South Carolina Congressman Preston Brooks used a walking cane to beat up antislavery Massachusetts Senator Charles Sumner during a Senate session.

Why important? The attacks in Kansas and on the floor of the Senate showed the slavery issue was not going to be settled through compromise.

248. HEBERT HOOVER (1929–1933)

The Great Depression and World War II, 1929–1945

The Great Depression and World War II, 1929–1945

The event that triggered the Great Depression (**#246**) was the stock market crash in October 1929. During the 1920s the economy boomed but there was evidence of trouble ahead.

1) Overproduction of goods and crops lowered some prices below the profit level.

2) The government took a hands-off approach to business and the economy.

3) Credit buying was a new way to buy a first car or radio, but it put more people than ever in debt.

Why important? Despite the warning signs, almost no one predicted the crash.

Buildup to the Civil War

104. JOHN BROWN

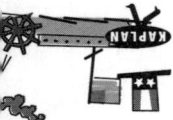

Brown led the most infamous attacks in "Bleeding Kansas" (**#103**). At Pottawatomie Creek Brown and his sons killed five pro-slavery settlers. He escaped prosecution and attempted to stage a slave revolt from Harper's Ferry, Virginia in 1859 (**#109**).

Why important? Despite his violent behavior, John Brown became a hero to some abolitionists, but many supporters of slavery saw his violent acts as representative of abolitionists in general and felt even more threatened.

247. CAUSES OF THE CRASH OF 1929

105. AMERICAN (KNOW-NOTHING) PARTY

The Great Depression and World War II, 1929–1945

The Great Depression was an international economic disaster that lasted from 1929 to 1940. At its worst in 1933, the unemployment rate was 25%. Banks and other businesses failed in record numbers.

Why important? The Great Depression was the worst economic crisis in American history and led to many long-lasting political, economic, and social changes, such as the New Deal (#251).

Buildup to the Civil War

This short-lived third party of the 1850s opposed further immigration and the spread of Catholicism. Supporters feared that immigrants were taking jobs that belonged to Americans who were already here, and they feared that growing numbers of Catholics, particularly from Ireland, threatened the Protestant majority. When it came to other political and social questions, members of this party often said they "knew nothing."

Why important? The debate over the number of immigrants allowed into the United States has continued throughout American history.

▲ 246. GREAT DEPRESSION

The Great Depression and World War II, 1929–1945

106. REPUBLICAN PARTY

In 1921, the Washington Conference called the world's naval powers together to discuss disarmament. In 1928, nations from around the world attempted to avoid future world war by signing the Kellogg-Briand Pact. It outlawed force as a foreign policy device.

Why important? It is often argued that after World War I America retreated from the world stage, but the Washington Conference and the Kellogg-Briand Pact suggest otherwise.

Buildup to the Civil War

This party was founded in 1854 in reaction against the passage of the Kansas-Nebraska Act (**#101**), by members of the Democrats and the Whigs who opposed the spread of slavery into new territories. Republicans basically had no support in the South. The first Republican president was Lincoln, elected in 1860.

Why important? The Republicans quickly became a major party, rivaling the Democrats as early as the 1856 presidential election. The party usually dominated all branches of the federal government from 1860 through the 1920s.

---

245. WASHINGTON CONFERENCE AND KELLOGG-BRIAND PACT

Wilson Era Through the 1920s, 1912–1929

▼ 107. *DRED SCOTT V. SANFORD*

Wilson Era Through the 1920s, 1912–1929

The Ku Klux Klan (KKK) faded in the South after the turn of the 20th century but by the 1920s it became more popular than before, expanding to all areas of the nation. Popular reaction against postwar change caused the KKK to target not only African Americans, but also immigrants, communists, Catholics, and Jews.

Why important? This is a counterexample to the supposedly progressive nature of the "Roaring '20s" (#234).

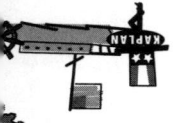

This controversial 1857 Supreme Court case struck down the Missouri Compromise (**#67**), allowing slavery to expand in the "free" territories of the North and West. Scott was a slave who was forced to accompany his master from Missouri to the free territory of Wisconsin in the 1830s. Once back in Missouri and after his master's death, Scott sued for freedom, arguing that he shouldn't have been a slave in Wisconsin since it did not permit slavery. Chief Justice Roger Taney not only sided with the majority against Scott, but also overturned the Missouri Compromise, claiming it deprived slave owners the right to own property wherever they chose.

Why important? This was another big step toward the Civil War. Slavery supporters rejoiced while abolitionists fumed.

244. REVIVAL OF THE KKK

Wilson Era Through the 1920s, 1912–1929

The 1920s saw reaction against radical politics (#233) and the huge influx of immigrants. The number of immigrants allowed into the United States was greatly curtailed and immigration of Japanese people was banned. Sacco and Vanzetti were immigrant radicals who were convicted of murder and robbery, and executed.

Why important? Some say Sacco and Vanzetti were innocent but were executed in a symbolic backlash against unpopular ideas and immigration.

108. LINCOLN-DOUGLAS DEBATES

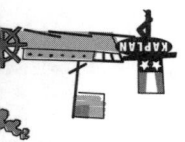

In the 1858 Illinois senate election, Republican candidate Abraham Lincoln challenged the incumbent Democrat, Senator Stephen A. Douglas (**#102**), to a series of debates, which were mostly about slavery. Despite an excellent showing in the debates, including his famous "House Divided" speech, Lincoln lost the election.

Why important? This election was covered by the national press and Lincoln became famous . . . and the president in 1860.

243. SACCO AND VANZETTI

Wilson Era Through the 1920s, 1912–1929

In 1925 in Dayton, Tennessee, John Scopes was put on trial for teaching evolution in a public school, against state law. Politician William Jennings Bryan and famous defense lawyer Clarence Darrow squared off. Scopes was found guilty as charged and was fined $100.

Why important? Though Scopes lost, over time all states allowed evolution to be taught in public schools. Today the argument is over whether creationism should be taught.

109. HARPER'S FERRY, VIRGINIA

Buildup to the Civil War

Buildup to the Civil War

In 1859, John Brown (**#104**) and followers tried to start a slave revolt. To get weapons they attacked an arsenal in Harper's Ferry, Virginia. Brown's plan was to arm local slaves, and as word spread of this revolt, for slaves throughout the South to rebel and claim their freedom. Colonel Robert E. Lee led the U.S. Army's capture of Brown, who was tried and hanged for treason. **Why important?** This violent outbreak brought the country closer to civil war. With his death, Brown became a martyr to the abolitionist cause.

242. SCOPES MONKEY TRIAL

Wilson Era Through the 1920s, 1912–1929

110. ELECTION OF 1860

In Harlem, New York in the 1920s, a boom in creativity in music and literature arose among the African-American community. Langston Hughes and Zora Neale Hurston were famous writers; Duke Ellington and Louis Armstrong (of New Orleans) were two of several outstanding jazz musicians.

Why important? In the early 20th century, black and white social worlds had little to do with one another, but both flourished in cultural creation at this time.

Buildup to the Civil War

The Democrats split over slavery. The Southern Democrats ran the current Vice President John C. Breckinridge of Kentucky, and Northern Democrats ran Senator Stephen A. Douglas of Illinois (**#102**). Abraham Lincoln of Illinois was the Republican nominee. A fourth group, the Constitutional Union Party, which favored attempting more compromises over slavery, ran John Bell of Tennessee. Despite not appearing on the ballot in most slave states, Lincoln won a majority of the electoral votes but only 40% of the popular vote.

Why important? South Carolina and other slave states threatened to secede if Lincoln, wrongly seen as an abolitionist, was elected.

---

241. HARLEM RENAISSANCE

Wilson Era Through the 1920s, 1912–1929

Wilson Era Through the 1920s, 1912–1929

Many great American writers emerged in the 1920s. The “Lost Generation” wrote about disenchantment during the postwar era of economic growth. F. Scott Fitzgerald most famously wrote about being rich in material goods but poor in spirit. William Faulkner, Ernest Hemingway, and Eugene O’Neill also were famous writers of the time.

Why important? American literature reached its peak in world popularity and respect.

---

111. SECESSION

Buildup to the Civil War

After the victory of Republican Abraham Lincoln in the presidential election of 1860, South Carolina broke from the Union. Six other slave states in the Deep South soon followed (Florida, Georgia, Alabama, Missouri, Louisiana, and Texas). With South Carolina, they formed the Confederate States of America (**#114**). After war broke out at Fort Sumter in April 1861 (**#116**), Virginia, North Carolina, Tennessee, and Arkansas joined the Confederacy.

Why important? States threatened to leave the Union over the War of 1812 (**#63**) and during the Nullification Crisis (**#79**), but in late 1860 and early 1861, they actually did.

240. LITERATURE OF THE 1920s

Wilson Era Through the 1920s, 1912–1929

112. CRITTENDEN COMPROMISE

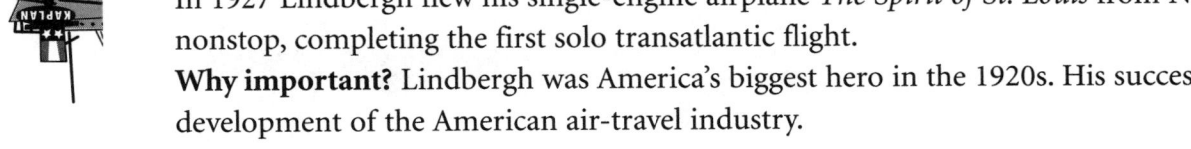

In 1927 Lindbergh flew his single-engine airplane *The Spirit of St. Louis* from New York to Paris nonstop, completing the first solo transatlantic flight.

Why important? Lindbergh was America's biggest hero in the 1920s. His success sparked the development of the American air-travel industry.

After the first 7 slave states left the Union, Kentucky Senator John Crittenden proposed an amendment to the U.S. Constitution that guaranteed slavery below the Missouri Compromise line. It failed.

Why important? This was a classic case of "too little, too late." By December 1860, compromise was the last thing on the minds of both pro- and antislavery factions.

---

239. CHARLES LINDBERGH

Wilson Era Through the 1920s, 1912–1929

Buildup to the Civil War

113. BORDER STATES

Wilson Era Through the 1920s, 1912–1929

Republicans owned the White House all through the 1920s. Generally, they did not intervene in the economy during this era of boom.

Why important? Historians believe the hands-off economic approach of the 1920s presidents contributed to the severity of the Great Depression (#246).

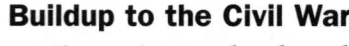

Four states permitted slavery but did not join the Confederacy: Kentucky, Missouri, Maryland, and Delaware.

Why important? The fact that four slave states chose to remain in the Union was a moral victory for Lincoln and a strategic loss for the Confederacy in the Civil War.

238. REPUBLICAN ECONOMIC POLICY IN THE 1920s

114. CONFEDERATE STATES OF AMERICA

Republican Warren G. Harding was elected president in 1920. His administration is known mostly for its scandals. In the most famous, Secretary of the Interior Albert Fall took bribes over oil leases on government-owned land in Wyoming called "Teapot Dome." Harding was not implicated in the scandals. He died before serving a complete term.

Why important? The Harding, Grant (**#155**), and Nixon (**#338**) administrations are generally regarded as the most corrupt.

This was the government of the 11 states that seceded from the Union. Its constitution was based on the Articles of Confederation (**#47**), therefore the individual states had more power than the national government. The capital was Montgomery, Alabama until it was moved to Richmond, Virginia in May 1861. Slavery was guaranteed in its constitution.

Why important? The Confederacy conducted the war effort for the South but was never recognized by the United States, or by any foreign nation.

237. HARDING SCANDALS

Ford did not invent the automobile but was its most successful producer. He lowered the price of his cars through the mass-production technique of the assembly line. His best-known car was the Model T.

Why important? The popularity of the car changed cities (people could live on the outskirts of town and drive to work; cities grew) and enhanced or created whole industries like steel, road construction, gas stations, and tourism.

115. JEFFERSON DAVIS

Davis was the only president of the Confederacy. A Mississippi senator, he was secretary of war (now defense) in the cabinet of President Franklin Pierce.

Why important? Davis led the Confederacy's war effort in the Civil War.

236. HENRY FORD

Wilson Era Through the 1920s, 1912–1929

For most job holders, real income increased in the 1920s. At the same time, prices fell for many goods because of mass-production techniques. One result was credit buying, where new products like cars, radios, and refrigerators were bought on the "installment plan": for a little money down and a little per month. Farmers, however, saw the price of agricultural products, and their profits, fall during the decade.

Why important? The combination of credit buying and falling farm prices led to the Great Depression (#246).

116. FORT SUMTER

Civil War and Reconstruction

After secession (**#111**), most of the Army's coastal forts in the South were turned over to the Confederacy, but the fort in the Charleston, South Carolina harbor remained in Union hands. In April 1861, despite warnings from the Confederate government, Lincoln sent supplies to the Union troops in Fort Sumter. The Confederates fired cannons at the fort for 40 hours and the Union troops surrendered.

Why important? Fort Sumter was the site of the first shots of the Civil War. After Lincoln called for 90-day volunteers to put down the rebellion, the slave states of North Carolina, Tennessee, Virginia, and Arkansas seceded.

---

235. CONSUMER SOCIETY

Wilson Era Through the 1920s, 1912–1929

America emerged from World War I a world leader but many citizens were uncomfortable with that role. A "youth culture" emerged for the first time. Many young people dressed differently than their elders and listened to different music: jazz. The automobile made chaperoned courting impossible and began a new phenomenon: the date. Movies were a rising form of entertainment. Radio broadcast networks like NBC and CBS began mass entertainment. At the same time signs of resistance to change were seen in the Red Scare (**#233**) and the reemergence of the Ku Klux Klan (**#244**).

Why important? In the 20th century, the two eras that saw the most social change were the 1920s and 1960s.

117. GOALS OF NORTH AND SOUTH IN THE CIVIL WAR

The Confederacy's goal was to become an independent slaveholding country recognized by the United States and foreign powers. The initial goal of the United States was to restore the seceded states to the Union, but after the Emancipation Proclamation (**#124**) the goal of ending slavery was added.

Why important? Once the United States adopted emancipation as a reason for fighting the Civil War, it claimed the moral high ground in the conflict.

---

234. "ROARING '20s"

Wilson Era Through the 1920s, 1912–1929

▼ 118. ADVANTAGES OF NORTH AND SOUTH IN THE CIVIL WAR

Wilson Era Through the 1920s, 1912–1929

After Russia came under communist control during World War I, many Americans feared a communist revolution in the United States. Attorney General Palmer authorized FBI Special Agent J. Edgar Hoover to conduct raids against suspected communists and other subversives.

Why important? A second and more famous "Red Scare" occurred in the 1950s (#307). Hoover ran the FBI from 1924 to 1972.

Civil War and Reconstruction

The United States had a higher population, a better navy, more factories, more railroads, and more farmland, but the Confederate States had a higher percentage of people who supported its cause, was usually defending familiar ground, and had a greater military tradition.

Why important? The Confederacy had the advantage in a short war, but the Union's strengths helped it more in a long war.

▲ 233. RED SCARE

Wilson Era Through the 1920s, 1912–1929

119. FIRST BATTLE OF BULL RUN

This Republican senator led opposition to American participation in the League of Nations (#231).

Why important? George Washington's warning against "foreign entanglements" (#55) was still popular after World War I, but after World War II America did accept the leading role on the world stage.

The first big land battle of the Civil War took place on July 21, 1861, in Virginia. The Confederates won the battle.

Why important? This victory made the Confederacy overly confident in its abilities to win the war, and caused many Union generals to consistently overestimate the power of Confederate forces in future battles.

232. HENRY CABOT LODGE

Wilson Era Through the 1920s, 1912–1929

Though it was one of his 14 points (**#230**), Wilson failed to convince Congress that America should participate in a League of Nations.

Why important? Wilson came up with the idea of an international organization and talked other countries into joining it, but America never joined. During his campaign to get Congress to sign on, Wilson had a stroke and became incapacitated for the rest of his presidency. The League of Nations was the precursor to the United Nations (**#294**).

---

120. ANACONDA PLAN

Civil War and Reconstruction

Union general-in-chief Winfield Scott planned to isolate the Confederacy via several steps. 1) The U.S. Navy would blockade the South's ports to keep it from trading with foreign nations. 2) The Union would take control of the Mississippi River (thereby cutting the South off from the West). 3) Scott would raise a large Union army and take the Confederate capital at Richmond, Virginia. 4) The Union army would divide the South by capturing the Tennessee River Valley and marching through Georgia to the coast.

Why important? Unlike most Union strategists, Scott made plans for a long war, and he was proven correct.

▲ 231. LEAGUE OF NATIONS (1919)

Wilson proposed a peace settlement in World War I based on 14 items including an international organization to prevent future wars (League of Nations) (**#231**), freedom of people to choose their own government ("self-determination"), and an end to secret treaties between nations. When the "Big Four" leaders from the United States, England, France, and Italy met, Wilson had to compromise on his "peace without victory" ideals (**#225**) because England and France demanded punishment of Germany.

Why important? The harsh demands put on Germany in the Treaty of Versailles led to resentment, economic difficulties, and World War II.

121. BATTLE OF ANTIETAM

Civil War and Reconstruction

In September 1862, Confederate general Robert E. Lee invaded Maryland, hoping a victory would convince that state to join the Confederacy. At Antietam, Union and Confederate forces fought to a tie, but Lee withdrew to Virginia after the battle.

Why important? This was the bloodiest day of the war (22,000 killed or wounded). Heartened by Lee's retreat, Lincoln issued the Emancipation Proclamation (**#124**), effective January 1863. Maryland remained in the Union.

230. 14 POINTS (1918) AND TREATY OF VERSAILLES (1919)

The Selective Service Act created a military draft, adding almost 3 million men to the armed forces. Job opportunities for women and African Americans opened up during the war. Both worked in factories that were mostly in northern cities.

Why important? African-American migration north increased dramatically. As a sort of "thank you" to women, Congress approved the 19th Amendment **(#220)** after the war. Women worked in factories in even greater numbers in World War II.

122. BLOODY SHILOH

Civil War and Reconstruction

In western Tennessee in April 1862, the Union achieved a difficult victory in heavy fighting. A total of 23,000 were killed or wounded in two days.

Why important? This battle, part of the Union strategy to take the Mississippi River, was the bloodiest in the "West," a term used to describe all fighting west of the Appalachian Mountains.

229. SOCIAL EFFECTS OF WORLD WAR I

Wilson Era Through the 1920s, 1912–1929

123. *MONITOR* VS. *MERRIMAC*

Pershing led the American Expeditionary Force in World War I. When the Americans arrived in France, Pershing supposedly said, "Lafayette, we are here." This meant the United States was paying back France for its help in the American Revolution.

Why important? French and English commanders wanted to put all U.S. forces under their control, but Pershing showed American independence when he held firm against that idea.

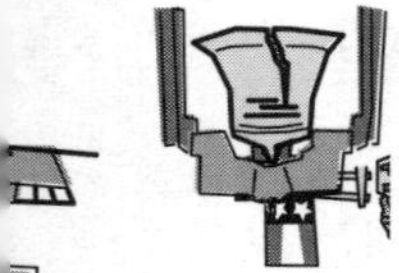

Civil War and Reconstruction

Two ships, the U.S.S. *Monitor* and the C.S.S. *Merrimac*, battled each other near Hampton Roads, Virginia in March 1862. Neither was a clear winner.

Why important? This was the first "clash of ironclads"—ships covered in iron, not just wood—and marked the beginning of modern naval design.

228. JOHN J. "BLACKJACK" PERSHING

Wilson Era Through the 1920s, 1912–1929

124. EMANCIPATION PROCLAMATION

President Wilson authorized government programs to "talk up" America's participation in World War I. George Creel headed the Committee on Public Information, which produced anti-German propaganda and paid actors to promote the war effort.

Why important? This was a precursor to the even bigger government-sponsored effort that promoted America's involvement in World War II.

After the battle of Antietam (**#121**), President Lincoln announced that on January 1, 1863, slaves would be free in all areas in rebellion against the United States.

Why important? The Emancipation Proclamation shifted the main reason for the Civil War from reunification with the South to freedom for the slaves. It got the attention of important foreign opponents of slavery like England, which voted to not recognize the Confederacy.

227. COMMITTEE ON PUBLIC INFORMATION

Wilson Era Through the 1920s, 1912–1929

125. VICKSBURG CAMPAIGN

Wilson Era Through the 1920s, 1912–1929

Representative Jeanette Rankin and Senator Robert LaFollette (#211) voted against America's entry into World War I.

Why important? Rankin was the first female member of Congress and a committed pacifist. She also voted against declaring war on Japan in World War II.

In July 1863, after a long campaign to take the Mississippi River out of Confederate control, Union general Ulysses S. Grant's forces obtained the surrender of Vicksburg, Mississippi. A few days later, the Confederate army downriver at Port Hudson, Louisiana gave up as well, prompting Lincoln to write, "The father of waters again goes unvexed to the sea."

Why important? With these victories, one phase of the Anaconda Plan (**#120**) was complete.

226. JEANETTE RANKIN

Wilson Era Through the 1920s, 1912–1929

126. BATTLE OF GETTYSBURG

Wilson Era Through the 1920s, 1912–1929

In his speech to Congress asking for a declaration of war, Wilson promoted "peace without victory" and said the real reason for America's entry into World War I was to "make the world safe for democracy." In other words, America was in the war to promote democracy among the monarchies of Europe and to save Europe from itself.

Why important? Wilson's noble words were strongly tested in the peace settlement of WWI (#230). World War I marked a major turning point in American foreign policy.

Civil War and Reconstruction

This battle involved the most soldiers and produced the most deaths in the Civil War. In July 1863, Confederate general Robert E. Lee's army marched into southern Pennsylvania. In three days of fighting over 50,000 soldiers were killed or wounded and Lee retreated to Virginia. In November, Lincoln gave his famous Gettysburg Address at the dedication of the national cemetery there. **Why important?** The Battle of Gettysburg was the turning point of the Civil War. Lincoln's speech is widely considered the greatest in American history.

225. "MAKE THE WORLD SAFE FOR DEMOCRACY"

Wilson Era Through the 1920s, 1912–1929

Civil War and Reconstruction

127. COPPERHEADS

Wilson Era Through the 1920s, 1912–1929

In 1917, Germany sent a telegram to the Mexican government encouraging it to attack the United States. Germany also said it was going to return to "unrestricted submarine warfare," meaning it was going to sink any vessel bound for England. This included American ships, even though America claimed to be neutral.

Why important? As a result, Wilson asked Congress to declare war on Germany. It did and the United States entered World War I.

Antiwar citizens of the Union were called Copperheads, after the poisonous snake. Some Copperheads were openly pro-Confederate.

Why important? The existence of the Copperheads showed that in the Union support for the war was not universal. There were even anti-draft riots in New York City in 1863.

224. ZIMMERMAN TELEGRAM

Wilson Era Through the 1920s, 1912–1929

▼ 128. SHERMAN'S MARCH TO THE SEA

This leader of Mexican revolutionaries crossed into Texas and New Mexico in 1916 and killed several Americans. President Wilson sent the army, led by General Pershing (**#228**), to find Villa. It failed to do so.

Why important? The pursuit of Villa gave Pershing experience leading an army in the field just before the United States entered World War I.

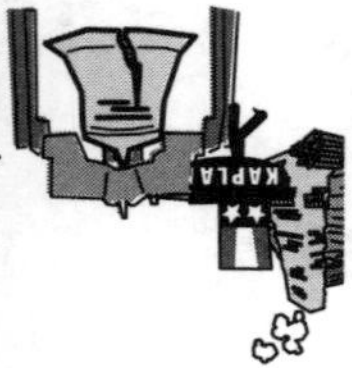

Civil War and Reconstruction

Union general William Tecumseh Sherman believed the best way to end the war as soon as possible was to be as destructive as possible, depriving the Confederacy of the materials and will it needed to keep going. Sherman's army marched "to the sea" from Chattanooga, Tennessee to Savanna, Georgia, destroying everything in its path.

Why important? Sherman's strategy marked the beginning of the doctrine of total war, under which soldiers and civilians alike are considered legitimate targets.

223. PANCHO VILLA

Wilson Era Through the 1920s, 1912–1929

129. APPOMATTOX COURT HOUSE

World War I started in Europe in 1914. The majority of Americans wanted to stay out of it, even though most were of European descent. Wilson won reelection in 1916 using this campaign slogan.

Why important? This shows that even into the 20th century, most Americans followed George Washington's advice to stay out of foreign entanglements (#55).

Civil War and Reconstruction

The Confederate capital, Richmond, Virginia, fell to Union forces in April 1865. On April 9, 1865, Confederate general Robert E. Lee surrendered to Union general Ulysses S. Grant at Appomattox Court House in southwest Virginia.

Why important? Lee's surrender marked the last major campaign of the Confederacy in the Civil War.

---

222. "HE KEPT US OUT OF WAR"

Wilson Era Through the 1920s, 1912–1929

130. RESULTS OF THE CIVIL WAR

Wilson Era Through the 1920s, 1912–1929

Besides the Progressive Amendments, other governmental innovations came about during the Progressive era. 1) The Federal Reserve System was created, reorganizing how currency is distributed around the country. 2) Initiative, referendum, and recall legislation gave voters more power in elections.

Why important? The Progressive movement **(#210)** went beyond party lines to influence Republicans and Democrats on local, state, and national levels in the first two decades of the 20th century.

Almost 620,000 Americans died. Lincoln was assassinated just after the war's end. Almost four million slaves were freed, but their place in American society remained unclear for decades. The Union was restored during the Reconstruction era (**#131**). The power of the federal government increased. No state seriously threatened to secede again. The industrial revolution, begun after the War of 1812 and involving railroads and other manufacturing sectors (**#69, #72, #89**), was greatly accelerated.

Why important? All of the events cited above had major, lasting impacts on American society.

▲ 221. PROGRESSIVE LEGISLATION

Wilson Era Through the 1920s, 1912–1929

Many changes were made to the U.S. Constitution during the Progressive era. The 16th Amendment (1913) created a national income tax. The 17th Amendment (1913) began the election of senators by popular vote—previously, senators were picked by state legislatures. The 18th Amendment (1919) made selling or drinking alcohol illegal. The 19th Amendment (1920) allowed women to vote in national elections.

Why important? These amendments show the popularity of the Progressive agenda (**#210**) at the beginning of the 20th century.

131. RECONSTRUCTION

Civil War and Reconstruction

From 1865 to 1877, the states of the Confederacy were brought back into the Union. Congress and the presidents of this era clashed over the proper method of restoration.

Why important? Reconstruction was a difficult transitional era that saw a great deal of political fighting over the use of power by the national government.

▲ 220. PROGRESSIVE AMENDMENTS

Wilson Era Through the 1920s, 1912–1929

In 1912, Theodore Roosevelt failed in an attempt to take the Republican nomination from President Taft. Roosevelt's supporters split with the Republicans and formed the Bull Moose Party ("I'm as fit as a bull moose!" claimed Roosevelt). In the election, Roosevelt ran second to Democrat Woodrow Wilson and Taft finished third.

Why important? This was the strongest showing of any third party in a presidential election in American history. With Wilson's victory, Democrats became the more liberal party and Republicans more conservative, a trend that continues.

132. LINCOLN-JOHNSON PLAN

Also known as the 10% Plan, this was Lincoln's (and later, President Andrew Johnson's) plan to restore the Confederate states to the Union. Lincoln proposed that pardons go to ex-Confederates who 1) pledged their allegiance to the United States and 2) accepted the end of slavery. When at least 10% of the former Confederates did so, the state could write a new constitution outlawing slavery, and new representatives could be sent to Congress.

Why important? Opposition to this lenient plan quickly arose in Congress, leading to unprecedented battles between the legislative and executive branches of government.

---

219. BULL MOOSE PARTY

Theodore Roosevelt Era, 1898–1912

133. WADE-DAVIS BILL

This was an important third party of the early 20th century. The Socialists insisted on even more government involvement in the economy than the Progressives (**#210**), with proposals like government ownership of most major industries. The party leader was Eugene Debs (**#180**).

Why important? The Socialists made the Progressives look moderate by comparison, so the latter group gained in popularity.

Civil War and Reconstruction

To counter the Lincoln-Johnson Plan (**#132**), in 1864 Congress approved this bill, which tightened the rules allowing ex-Confederate states back into the Union. Instead of 10%, 50% of a state's voters had to take a loyalty oath and no one from the former Confederate army could vote for a new state constitution. Lincoln refused to sign the bill, so it failed.

Why important? This was an early example of the battles to come between president and Congress during Reconstruction.

218. SOCIALIST PARTY

Theodore Roosevelt Era, 1898–1912

134. FREEDMEN'S BUREAU

Roosevelt's successor, William Howard Taft, supported developing American influence overseas through business and trade rather than with Roosevelt's style of military intimidation.

Why important? U.S. foreign policy since Theodore Roosevelt has often shifted between the two views represented by Roosevelt and Taft: military force or economic incentives.

Civil War and Reconstruction

Congress created this government agency in March 1865 to help freed slaves and destitute whites recover from the war by providing food, clothing, and shelter. Most famously, schools were built throughout the South to educate ex-slaves. President Johnson vetoed a provision in the Freedmen's Bureau bill to give land to ex-slaves, commonly called "forty acres and a mule."

Why important? Despite its mixed successes, this was the federal government's first welfare agency—a sign of the growing power of the national government after the Civil War.

217. DOLLAR DIPLOMACY

Theodore Roosevelt Era, 1898–1912

135. RADICAL REPUBLICANS

Theodore Roosevelt Era, 1898–1912

As president, Theodore Roosevelt saw himself as a defender of the "little guy" against the corporate giants of the day. At the time a "trust" was a name for a large corporation that had a monopoly in an industry. Roosevelt enforced the Sherman Antitrust Act (**#169**) and split up Rockefeller's Standard Oil, as well as the Northern Securities railroad monopoly. President Taft did even more trust-busting than Roosevelt.

Why important? This was yet another sign of increased government involvement in the economy.

Civil War and Reconstruction

Radical Republicans were opponents of the Lincoln-Johnson Plan for Reconstruction. Leaders like Thaddeus Stevens, Benjamin Wade, and Charles Sumner sought to treat the former Confederate states like conquered provinces to be occupied by U.S. military forces until Congress readmitted the states. **Why important?** The Radicals won many Congressional seats in the 1866 elections and dominated Reconstruction policy for years.

216. TRUST-BUSTING

Theodore Roosevelt Era, 1898–1912

136. CONGRESSIONAL RECONSTRUCTION

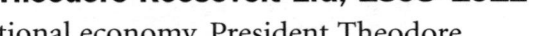

Theodore Roosevelt Era, 1898–1912

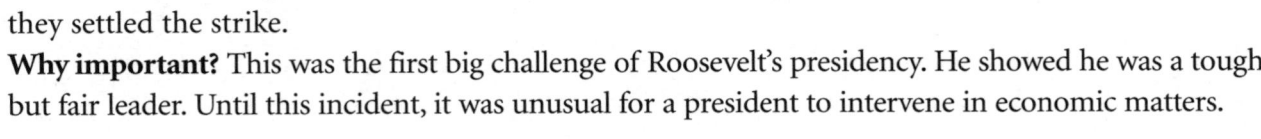

In 1902 a strike by coal miners threatened to harm the national economy. President Theodore Roosevelt called strike leaders and mine owners to the White House and told them to settle the strike or watch him put soldiers to work in the mines. Believing that he was a man of his word, they settled the strike.

Why important? This was the first big challenge of Roosevelt's presidency. He showed he was a tough but fair leader. Until this incident, it was unusual for a president to intervene in economic matters.

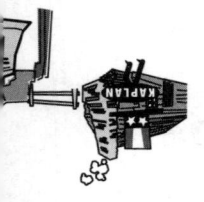

President Andrew Johnson angered many members of Congress by vetoing several Reconstruction bills. Led by the Radical Republicans (**#135**), Congress in 1867 voted to end the Lincoln-Johnson Plan (**#132**) and place the states of the former Confederacy under military control.

Why important? Struggles between the president and Congress were particularly harsh during Reconstruction. In addition, many whites in the South resented the harsh nature of Congressional Reconstruction and took out their anger on ex-slaves, using political, social, and economic tactics.

215. ANTHRACITE COAL STRIKE

Theodore Roosevelt Era, 1898–1912

137. "CIVIL WAR AMENDMENTS"

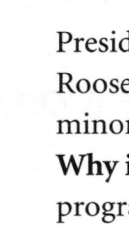

Theodore Roosevelt Era, 1898–1912

President Theodore Roosevelt named his agenda of Progressive reform the "Square Deal." Roosevelt promoted votes for women, government regulation of big business, and civil rights for minorities, especially African Americans.

Why important? Roosevelt was the first of several presidents who created ambitious domestic programs like the New Deal (**#251**), the Fair Deal (**#300**), and the Great Society (**#326**).

This name is commonly applied to the 13th, 14th, and 15th Amendments to the U.S. Constitution. The 13th (1865) ended slavery; the 14th (1868) defined a citizen as anyone born in the United States and guaranteed "equal protection" to all citizens; and the 15th (1870) gave voting rights to black males.

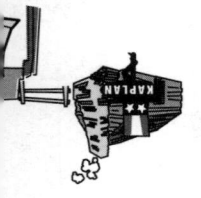

Why important? The elevation of American slaves from servitude to voting citizens took place in just five years. Debates continue over the meaning of "citizen" and "equal protection."

214. SQUARE DEAL

Theodore Roosevelt Era, 1898–1912

Theodore Roosevelt Era, 1898–1912

Politicians like Theodore Roosevelt read *The Jungle* (**#212**) and were moved to create government rules regarding labeling of packaged foods and drugs, as well as establish government inspection of meat processing plants to insure the safety of processed meats. Both the Pure Food and Drug Act and the Meat Inspection Act were passed in 1906.

Why important? The tiny print on the side of a can of soup and the label "USDA Inspected" on meat and dairy products are the result of this step of increased government regulation of business.

138. IMPEACHMENT

Civil War and Reconstruction

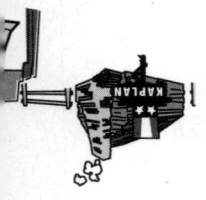

In 1867 Congress passed the Tenure of Office Act, which said that the president couldn't fire anyone without congressional approval. Johnson deliberately violated this law to challenge its constitutionality. In 1868 Radical Republicans tried to get rid of President Johnson by charging him with "high crimes and misdemeanors" in a procedure called "impeachment." Johnson was found not guilty by a slim vote in Congress.

Why important? Impeachment does not mean conviction, but instead a bringing of charges and a trial. Presidents Johnson and Clinton (**#347**) both were impeached, but neither was convicted. However, the effectiveness of both presidents diminished afterward.

---

213. PURE FOOD AND DRUG ACT, MEAT INSPECTION ACT

Theodore Roosevelt Era, 1898–1912

Theodore Roosevelt Era, 1898–1912

These investigative journalists in the Progressive era (**#210**) exposed political corruption, unethical business practices (Ida Tarbell, *The History of the Standard Oil Company*; Frank Norris's novel, *The Octopus*), poor housing conditions (Jacob Riis, *How the Other Half Lives*), and unsafe food processing (Upton Sinclair's novel, *The Jungle*).

Why important? These and other works swayed the public into pushing the government to step in and make changes (**#213**) . . . something it hadn't done much of before.

---

139. CARPETBAGGERS AND SCALAWAGS

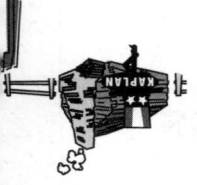

These were nicknames given to supporters of Reconstruction. Southerners called Northerners who moved South during Reconstruction "carpetbaggers" (a carpetbag was a type of suitcase). "Scalawags" were even worse—they were Southerners who supported the carpetbaggers (on a farm, a scalawag was a useless animal).

Why important? The use of these derisive names shows the resentment many Southerners had toward Reconstruction.

▲ 212. MUCKRAKERS

Theodore Roosevelt Era, 1898–1912

140. SHARECROPPING

LaFollette was a founder of the Progressive movement (**#210**). He served as governor of Wisconsin, senator from Wisconsin, and ran as the Progressive Party candidate for president in 1924.

Why important? LaFollette's "Wisconsin Idea" of higher taxes on the wealthy, increased funds for public schools, and more government regulation of railroad rates was championed by Progressive Party leaders around the United States.

Civil War and Reconstruction

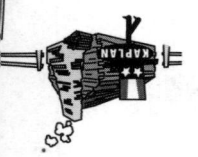

After the Civil War many ex-slaves continued to work for their former owners in agricultural labor. Landowners provided materials and seed in exchange for roughly half of the harvest. Sharecroppers were usually paid in money that was good only at the landowner's private store. This system survived in some parts of the South until the 1960s.

Why important? With no land of their own, and very little widely accepted currency, sharecropping families were caught in an economic trap with few chances for advancement.

211. ROBERT LAFOLLETTE

Theodore Roosevelt Era, 1898–1912

Civil War and Reconstruction

141. KU KLUX KLAN

Theodore Roosevelt Era, 1898–1912

The Progressives of the early 20th century had many of the same goals as the Populists (#192), but instead of coming largely from farming interests, they were mainly from cities and generally better educated. The Progressive Party was a major third party, but when Democrats and Republicans adopted its ideas, its power faded.

Why important? The Progressives had more success than the Populists in getting legislation passed, including the 16th, 17th, 18th, and 19th Amendments (#220).

Civil War and Reconstruction

Some whites in the South resisted Reconstruction policies of racial equality by forming vigilante groups that terrorized black citizens. The most infamous was the Ku Klux Klan. The Klan tried to stop blacks from voting and from gaining economic independence.

Why important? Groups like the KKK succeeded in stopping the African-American vote in many parts of the North and South. It experienced a revival in the 1920s when it expanded its hatred to Catholics, Jews, and immigrants.

210. PROGRESSIVE PARTY

Theodore Roosevelt Era, 1898–1912

Civil War and Reconstruction

▼ 142. JIM CROW LAWS

Theodore Roosevelt Era, 1898–1912

President Roosevelt sent several new, bright white warships on an impressive cruise around the world (1907–1909).

Why important? This was another show of growing American might on the world stage.

These laws were enacted after the Civil War, most prominently in the South, to deny civil rights to African Americans. "Black codes" forbade blacks from testifying against white citizens in court, made voting almost impossible, and strictly segregated white and black societies.

Why important? Despite their southern origin, laws that discriminated on account of race existed throughout the United States until the 1960s, helped by the 1896 Supreme Court ruling in *Plessy v. Ferguson* (**#158**).

209. GREAT WHITE FLEET

Theodore Roosevelt Era, 1898–1912

143. COMPROMISE OF 1877

Theodore Roosevelt Era, 1898–1912

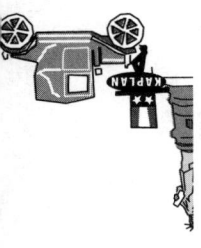

In 1904 President Theodore Roosevelt tacked a new policy onto the Monroe Doctrine (#68) when he told the world's nations—especially those of Europe—that if they had any problems with Latin American nations, they were to deal with the United States, which would act as an intermediary. This was especially true in financial matters.

Why important? America's claim to a "caretaker" role over its southern neighbors showed Europe it was a major international power. This attitude may have impressed the Europeans, but it angered many leaders and citizens in Latin America.

To settle the disputed 1876 presidential election, eventual winner Rutherford B. Hayes pledged to pull the last of the U.S. soldiers out of the three remaining "unreconstructed" states of the former Confederacy: South Carolina, Louisiana, and Florida.

Why important? Reconstruction ended, but in the South bitterness against its policies and practices remained.

208. ROOSEVELT COROLLARY

Theodore Roosevelt Era, 1898–1912

144. RECONSTRUCTION EVALUATED

Theodore Roosevelt Era, 1898–1912

During Theodore Roosevelt's presidency, the United States sent a show of military force to Colombia's coast, convincing that nation to cede territory to create the nation of Panama. The United States made a deal with the new Panamanian government to dig a canal through the country linking the Gulf of Mexico with the Pacific Ocean. The Panama Canal was constructed between 1904 and 1914. When finished, it provided an important trade route that bypassed the entire South American continent.

Why important? The Panama Canal was a source of great national pride in the United States and another sign of American ingenuity and power at the beginning of the 20th century. The United States relinquished control of the canal to Panama in 2000.

Civil War and Reconstruction

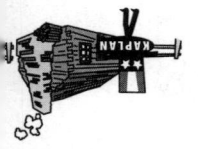

Positive effects of Reconstruction include the Civil War Amendments (**#137**), education provided for black students (**#134**), and the fact that former Confederate states were allowed back into the Union. Negative effects include the following: many promises made by the national government to ex-slaves went unfulfilled, civil rights laws were often ignored (**#141, #142**), some Southerners vented their frustration over Reconstruction policies with violence, and battles between Johnson and Congress led to his impeachment (**#138**).

Why important? The legacy of Reconstruction's failures regarding equal rights for African-American citizens affected U.S. society for over a century.

---

207. PANAMA CANAL

Theodore Roosevelt Era, 1898–1912

145. TURNER'S FRONTIER THESIS

In response to years of Western influence in China a group of nationalists called "Boxers" led an uprising throughout northeast China. While also targeting the outposts of other Western nations, the Boxers besieged the American embassy in Peking (Beijing) for 55 days in 1900. Multinational forces from the United States, Russia, Japan, and England put down the rebellion.

Why important? The Boxer Rebellion was another early example of American involvement in Asia—a sign of things to come in the 20th century.

Thirty Years of Change, 1865–1897

In 1893, historian Frederick Jackson Turner claimed that westward expansion explains the American character. The West provided a "safety valve" when population pressures became too great in Eastern cities. People searched for new opportunities "out West." Independence and "rugged individualism" were results of the steady migration of descendants of Europeans into the West.

Why important? In 1890 the U.S. Census Bureau officially declared the frontier closed, but the West remained prominent in American movies, novels, and television shows. This supports Turner's thesis.

206. BOXER REBELLION

Theodore Roosevelt Era, 1898–1912

146. SEWARD'S FOLLY

During the McKinley administration (**#195**), Secretary of State John Hay suggested to European powers and Japan that all countries with interests in China have equal access to trade in that country. Those nations agreed to go along with Hay's idea. Before this proposal, they had divided China into exclusive trading areas called "spheres of influence."

Why important? This was the first time a group of foreign powers accepted an American foreign policy idea, showing increased influence of the United States in world affairs.

In 1867, Secretary of State William Seward negotiated the purchase of Alaska from Russia. Opponents derided the deal as a big waste of the government's money, calling the territory "Seward's Folly" and "Seward's Icebox."

Why important? The critics were wrong. Not only did Alaska become a state—the largest—in 1959, but it was the site of an important gold rush in the 1890s and of oil reserves today. It also boasts beautiful wildlife and scenery.

▲ 205. OPEN-DOOR POLICY

Theodore Roosevelt Era, 1898–1912

After the Spanish-American War, America promised to recognize Cuba as an independent nation. However, with the Platt Amendment of 1901 the U.S. Congress forced Cuba to allow the United States to intervene in Cuban affairs whenever the United States thought it necessary. America also established a naval base in Cuba at Guantánamo Bay.

Why important? The United States became a "big brother" to Cuba for many years, until Fidel Castro took over in 1959 (**#322**).

147. *ALABAMA* CLAIMS

Thirty Years of Change, 1865–1897

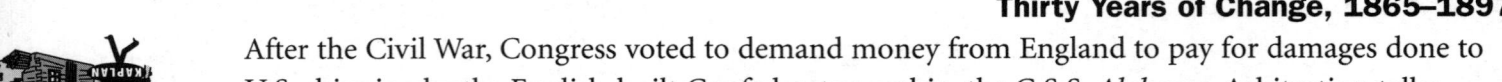

After the Civil War, Congress voted to demand money from England to pay for damages done to U.S. shipping by the English-built Confederate warship, the C.S.S. *Alabama*. Arbitration talks resulted in England paying the U.S. government $15 million in 1871.

Why important? By submitting to arbitration instead of going to war, the United States created a template for the peaceful settlement of future international disputes.

204. PLATT AMENDMENT

Theodore Roosevelt Era, 1898–1912

▼ 148. HOMESTEAD ACT (1862)

The Supreme Court ruled on the civil-rights status of the people living in the islands that America obtained in the Spanish-American War (**#196**), saying they were not full American citizens. "Insular" means "islands."

Why important? The Supreme Court's ruling was another part of America's controversial decision to become a participant in imperialism (**#197**).

Thirty Years of Change, 1865–1897

To promote the settlement of the Great Plains during the Civil War, Congress provided 160 acres of free land to any family that survived for five years.

Why important? The population of whites in the Great Plains region increased dramatically, transforming the West in many ways.

▲ 203. INSULAR CASES

Theodore Roosevelt Era, 1898–1912

Thirty Years of Change, 1865–1897

149. PACIFIC RAILWAY ACT

Theodore Roosevelt Era, 1898–1912

The United States added the Philippines to its territory after it took the Philippines from Spain in the Spanish-American War. Filipino fighters then rebelled against U.S. occupation because they had hoped to become an independent nation once Spain left. Emilio Aguinaldo led Filipino forces in an effort to expel the Americans, but after years of bloodshed, the Americans prevailed. **Why important?** This was the first war the United States fought in Asia, but not the last. America eventually granted the islands independence in 1947.

Thirty Years of Change, 1865–1897

In 1862 Congress approved funding for a Transcontinental Railroad to link California to the Mississippi River. The Central Pacific Railroad hired workers, many from China, to lay track from California to the east, and the Union Pacific Railroad put down track from Nebraska to the west. They met in 1869 in Utah.

Why important? The Transcontinental Railroad was the longest in the world at the time and was a source of great American pride. It also made it easier for even more settlers to move west.

Theodore Roosevelt Era, 1898–1912

202. PHILIPPINE INSURRECTION (1899–1913)

Theodore Roosevelt Era, 1898–1912

In 1898 Theodore Roosevelt organized a group of volunteers called the "Rough Riders" who fought in Cuba in the Spanish-American War. They famously charged up San Juan Hill and defeated a group of Spanish soldiers.

Why important? Roosevelt became a national war hero and was elected governor of New York and then vice president of the United States on his way to becoming one of America's most active presidents.

150. INDIAN WARS

Thirty Years of Change, 1865–1897

Thirty Years of Change, 1865–1897

From the 1860s to 1890 a series of battles broke out between Native Americans and the U.S. Army. Indians resented the loss of traditional lands to whites, the great reduction in animal populations because of the impact from the railroads, and U.S. government policies designed to limit the movement of Indians into "white" land. The most famous battle—and Indian victory—was at the Little Big Horn River in Montana in 1876.

Why important? Clashes between settlers and natives started in America in the earliest colonial days and ended only when native resistance seemed utterly futile in the late 19th century.

---

201. ROUGH RIDERS

Theodore Roosevelt Era, 1898–1912

Thirty Years of Change, 1865–1897

151. *A CENTURY OF DISHONOR*

Theodore Roosevelt Era, 1898–1912

At the beginning of the Spanish-American War (1898)(**#196**), Assistant Secretary of the Navy Theodore Roosevelt ordered U.S. Navy Commodore George Dewey, in Hong Kong, to attack the Spanish fleet in the Philippine Islands.

Why important? Dewey destroyed the Spanish fleet and America took the Philippines from Spain at the end of the war.

Thirty Years of Change, 1865–1897

Helen Hunt Jackson's 1881 book chronicled the history of failed U.S. policy toward Native Americans. One example was the U.S. government's policy of forcing Indian nations onto tracts of often-poor land called reservations. Most reservations were/are west of the Mississippi River. Reservation land belonged to everyone in the Indian nation, not individuals.

Why important? Jackson's book provided a point of view rarely found in that era—one of sympathy toward Indians and criticism of U.S. government policy.

200. COMMODORE GEORGE DEWEY

Theodore Roosevelt Era, 1898–1912

Theodore Roosevelt Era, 1898–1912

In the 1890s two major New York newspapers, the *Journal*, run by William Randolph Hearst, and the *World*, by Joseph Pulitzer, competed for readers by adding features like big headlines, sports pages, and especially, sensational stories. They helped escalate the Spanish-American War with stories of Spanish atrocities in Cuba.

Why important? The trend of attention-grabbing journalism started by Hearst and Pulitzer continues.

---

152. DAWES ACT

Thirty Years of Change, 1865–1897

Thirty Years of Change, 1865–1897

The Dawes Severalty Act of 1887 was a federal program that attempted to break up the reservation system by granting as much as 160 acres to individual Native American families. It was hoped that over time, Indians would assimilate into American society.

Why important? The Dawes Act turned out to be another U.S. policy failure in Indian matters, mainly because the land set aside for individual use wasn't enough to support successful cultivation. In a later reform attempt, U.S. citizenship was granted to all Native Americans in 1924.

199. YELLOW JOURNALISM

Theodore Roosevelt Era, 1898–1912

Thirty Years of Change, 1865–1897

153. WOUNDED KNEE MASSACRE

Theodore Roosevelt Era, 1898–1912

U.S. Navy Captain Alfred Mahan wrote this influential book in 1890. In it he claimed that the great powers in world history always had strong navies.

Why important? Imperialists like McKinley and Theodore Roosevelt were convinced by the thesis of this book and built a world-class U.S. Navy.

Thirty Years of Change, 1865–1897

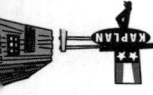

The Indian wars ended with the massacre of the Great Sioux Nation at Wounded Knee, South Dakota in 1890, the same year the U.S. government officially closed the frontier. Two hundred Native Americans were killed by U.S. soldiers.

Why important? The last major clash in the Indian Wars was a terrible end to hundreds of years of violent conflict.

198. THE INFLUENCE OF SEA POWER UPON HISTORY

Theodore Roosevelt Era, 1898–1912

Theodore Roosevelt Era, 1898–1912

From 1880 to 1914, European countries and America added territory around the world to their holdings. England and France were the two main players in Asia and Africa, while America concentrated on islands in the Caribbean and the Pacific.

Why important? By playing the imperial game with major world powers, America showed it was becoming a force to be reckoned with. National politics in 1900 centered over America's role in imperialism. The struggle for territory around the world helped lead to World War I.

154. GILDED AGE

Thirty Years of Change, 1865–1897

Thirty Years of Change, 1865–1897

Mark Twain coined this term to describe the 1870s and 1880s. "Gilded" things have a thin layer of shiny gold on top but cheap metal underneath.

Why important? This time period is usually remembered for the great wealth that developed because of new industries, but many in society still lived hard lives.

▲ 197. IMPERIALISM

Theodore Roosevelt Era, 1898–1912

▼ 155. POST-CIVIL WAR SCANDALS

Theodore Roosevelt Era, 1898–1912

By the 1890s many Cubans wanted independence from Spain. America wanted to help. In 1898, America declared war on Spain after the U.S.S. *Maine* exploded in Havana's harbor. In three months, America won the war and claimed the Philippine Islands, Puerto Rico, and Guam. Cuba became independent.

Why important? America joined the European trend of imperialism (#197) and became a world power.

Thirty Years of Change, 1865–1897

Political corruption reached new levels during the 1870s and 1880s. The Credit Mobilier scandal involved bribes given to politicians to get support for railroad companies—especially the Transcontinental Railroad. The Whiskey Ring bribed politicians so they wouldn't investigate tax fraud from whiskey makers. "Boss" Tweed stole millions from New York City taxpayers for himself and friends. Financiers Jay Gould and Jim Fisk paid friends close to President Grant in an attempt to control the nation's gold supply.

Why important? In the post-Civil War era corruption boomed as huge amounts of money were generated by the rapidly growing industrial revolution.

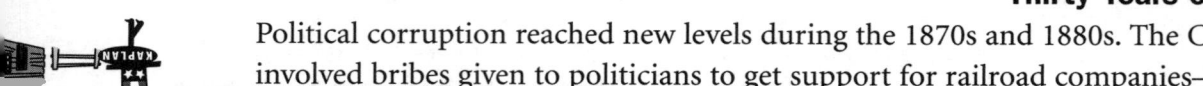

196. SPANISH-AMERICAN WAR (1898)

Theodore Roosevelt Era, 1898–1912

The Republicans retook the White House in 1896 when Ohio senator McKinley defeated Bryan. **Why important?** McKinley was president during the Spanish-American War, when the United States emerged as a major world power. He was assassinated in his second term and replaced by Theodore Roosevelt.

156. THOMAS NAST

Nast was a groundbreaking political cartoonist of the Gilded Age (**#154**). He exposed corruption in New York (**#155**) and in national politics through his newspaper cartoons. He also created the fat, jolly Santa Claus, the Democratic donkey, and the Republican elephant.

Why important? Nast proved that political cartoons could be a strong check against government corruption. His drawings effectively got the public's attention and fostered change.

195. WILLIAM MCKINLEY

Thirty Years of Change, 1865–1897

157. GEORGE WASHINGTON CARVER (1864–1943)

In 1896, both the Populists and the Democrats nominated Nebraska Congressman William Jennings Bryan. In his most famous speech, Bryan promoted the popular idea that the government should set the price of silver to one-sixteenth that of gold and pour millions of silver coins into circulation to help mining and farming interests. He said, "You shall not crucify mankind upon a cross of gold."

Why important? The Democrats took away the Populists' biggest issue (silver coinage) and the power of the Populist Party weakened. The price of silver never was linked to gold, however.

Carver was an African American who emphasized the application of scientific research to agriculture. From experiments at the Tuskegee Institute in Alabama, Carver developed hundreds of uses for agricultural products.

Why important? His most vital contribution was convincing farmers to rotate specific crops to renew soil nutrients that had disappeared from years of planting a single crop like cotton or tobacco.

194. "CROSS OF GOLD"

In 1894, Populist Party leader Jacob Coxey led thousands of unemployed workers on a march to Washington, DC to demand the government spend money to provide jobs. They were turned away and the "army" disbanded.

Why important? Politicians worried that Coxey's army was a sign of increasing trouble. The two major parties began to listen more to the demands of the Populists.

158. *PLESSY V. FERGUSON*

Thirty Years of Change, 1865–1897

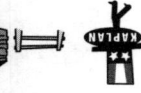

This 1896 Supreme Court ruling allowed “separate but equal” facilities for whites and blacks. **Why important?** In practice facilities were separate but almost never equal. This ruling revoked many of the gains promised to African Americans after the Civil War. *Plessy v. Ferguson* was finally overturned with the 1954 *Brown v. Board of Education* ruling (**#315**).

193. COXEY'S ARMY

Thirty Years of Change, 1865–1897

The Populist Party grew out of the National Farmers' Alliance (**#164**) and sought many of the same social and political goals. Its followers, mostly from the Midwest, wanted the following: 1) direct election of senators, 2) a graduated income tax, 3) an 8-hour workday, and 4) unlimited coinage of silver to get more money into circulation. In 1892 Populist candidate James Weaver received 22 electoral votes.

Why important? The Populist Party was one of the few third parties in American history that had long-lasting effects on national policies.

159. BOOKER T. WASHINGTON

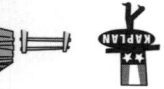

An African-American civil rights leader and educator who established the Tuskegee Institute, Washington famously argued in a speech at the Atlanta Exposition in 1895 that economic success and cooperation, not confrontation, were the keys to success for blacks. He was the first African American invited to dine at the White House (by Theodore Roosevelt).

Why important? Washington's stand on racial harmony clashed with that of W.E.B. DuBois (#160).

192. POPULIST PARTY

Thirty Years of Change, 1865–1897

160. W.E.B. DUBOIS

In the late 1880s, America reached out to countries to its south in the western hemisphere to develop cooperation in matters of trade and diplomacy. The organization formed out of this meeting was the Pan-American Union.

Why important? This was one of the first attempts the United States made to establish diplomatic ties with its southern neighbors. The Pan-American Union is now part of the Organization of American States (OAS).

This African-American leader cofounded the National Association for the Advancement of Colored People (NAACP) in 1908. DuBois argued that the time for cooperation with the white majority had passed and that boycotts and other proactive measures were needed. He was also a founder of the Niagara Movement, a precursor to the NAACP.

Why important? DuBois's open conflict with Booker T. Washington (**#159**) reflected the two main philosophies regarding the best way for blacks to obtain social equality in America.

191. PAN-AMERICAN CONFERENCE

161. SOCIAL DARWINISM

After President Garfield was assassinated by a disgruntled office seeker, Congress passed this act establishing the Civil Service Commission in 1883. The commission created tests that applicants for government jobs had to take to be hired.

Why important? The idea behind civil-service reform was to limit patronage (politicians giving government jobs to friends) and to give jobs to better-qualified people.

Some business and political leaders applied Darwin's "survival of the fittest" concept to human societies, believing that superior civilizations or businesses naturally deserve to conquer weaker ones. For example, societies that do not have much technology or military strength should yield to those that do.

Why important? Social Darwinism was the philosophy behind the business tactics of the "robber barons" or moguls (**#165**) and America's participation in the Age of Imperialism (**#197**).

---

190. PENDLETON ACT

Thirty Years of Change, 1865–1897

Thirty Years of Change, 1865–1897

162. GRANGE MOVEMENT

Thirty Years of Change, 1865–1897

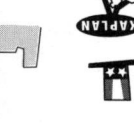

Cleveland was the only president to serve two nonconsecutive terms (1885–1889; 1893–1897) and the only Democrat who was elected president between 1860 and 1908.

Why important? During Cleveland's presidency the ICC was created (**#163**), the Pendleton Act was passed (**#190**), and the Panic of 1893 as well as the Pullman Strike (**#179**) occurred.

This was a sort of farmers' union, organized by Oliver H. Kelley in Washington, DC in 1868. It aimed to strengthen farmers' economic and political clout, but its influence faded by the 1880s. **Why important?** The Grange had success in getting some Midwestern state legislatures to regulate railroad freight charges and inspired later pro-farmer movements like the Populists (**#192**).

189. GROVER CLEVELAND

Thirty Years of Change, 1865–1897

163. INTERSTATE COMMERCE ACT

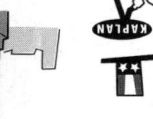

The Republican Party dominated national politics from 1860 to 1884. Three factions in the party were the Stalwarts, the Halfbreeds, and the Mugwumps. Stalwarts and Halfbreeds competed for power, political jobs, and sometimes bribes. The Mugwumps did not engage in this type of corruption and were less inclined to follow the party leaders.

Why important? "Halfbreed" President James Garfield was assassinated by a Stalwart. Mugwumps voted for Democrat Grover Cleveland (**#189**) in his first campaign in 1884.

In 1887, Congress passed a law that regulated railroad rates and created a federal oversight board, the Interstate Commerce Commission (ICC).

Why important? The ICC was the first of many federal regulatory commissions.

188. STALWARTS, HALFBREEDS, AND MUGWUMPS

Thirty Years of Change, 1865–1897

Thirty Years of Change, 1865–1897

For 30 years after the Civil War, Republican candidates won elections partly by blaming the Civil War on their Democrat opponents. Lincoln, the first assassinated president, was also the first Republican president.

Why important? Like the Vietnam War (#331), the Civil War had profound impact on American society and politics for decades after its end.

164. OCALA PLATFORM

Thirty Years of Change, 1865–1897

After the Grange movement (**#162**) faded, a new farmers' organization called the National Farmers' Alliance rose. At a meeting in Ocala, Florida in 1890 the National Alliance created a list of political changes that its members wanted, including: 1) direct election of U.S. senators, 2) a graduated income tax, 3) a revised federal banking system, and 4) increase of silver coinage into circulation.

Why important? These National Alliance ideas were adopted by the Populist (**#192**) and Progressive (**#210**) Parties and eventually became law.

187. WAVING THE BLOODY SHIRT

Thirty Years of Change, 1865–1897

165. MOGULS

The WCTU saw alcohol as one of America's greatest moral weaknesses and, with the Anti-Saloon League, worked to end its sale and consumption.

Why important? The efforts of these organizations led to the passage of the 18th Amendment in 1919, which prohibited the sale and consumption of alcohol (#220).

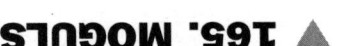

In the era after the Civil War, moguls were wealthy capitalist leaders who created the modern corporation and built huge commercial empires in railroads, steel, banking, petroleum, and shipping. **Why important?** Labeled by the public as either virtuous "captains of industry" or evil "robber barons," these men made American industries and financial institutions the largest in the world and gave millions of dollars to charities and other causes.

---

186. WOMEN'S CHRISTIAN TEMPERANCE UNION (WCTU)

The biggest trend in art and literature in this era was realism. Winslow Homer and Thomas Eakins were two important realist artists. Bret Harte and Mark Twain were internationally famous realist writers. As the century closed, European Impressionist paintings influenced the works of Mary Cassatt. Artists from the Ashcan school painted scenes from urban life. Naturalist writers like Stephen Crane, Jack London, and Upton Sinclair depicted American life in a straightforward manner.

Why important? American art and literature changed with the times and was admired around the world.

166. ANDREW CARNEGIE

Carnegie created the Carnegie Steel empire and gave generously to charities. He supported the Gospel of Wealth philosophy (**#171**). Carnegie used vertical integration (**#170**) in building his steel empire. He eventually sold his business to J.P. Morgan (**#167**).

Why important? Carnegie rose from being a poor immigrant to becoming one of the world's richest men, living the "American dream."

185. LATE 19TH CENTURY ART AND LITERATURE

Thirty Years of Change, 1865–1897

167. J.P. MORGAN

In the late 19th century, Addams became an advocate for women and immigrants. Her Hull House in Chicago was a "settlement house" that provided social services like education and support to immigrants.

Why important? Jane Addams inspired others to follow her example. Hundreds of settlement houses around the country provided assistance to those in need.

This wealthy banker and railroad owner created the largest corporation in the world, U.S. Steel, when he bought out Carnegie (**#166**). Morgan's banking skills were so great that the U.S. government borrowed money from him during the Panic of 1893.

Why important? U.S. Steel was the world's first billion-dollar company. J.P. Morgan's bank business is still a major financial corporation today.

184. JANE ADDAMS

Thirty Years of Change, 1865–1897

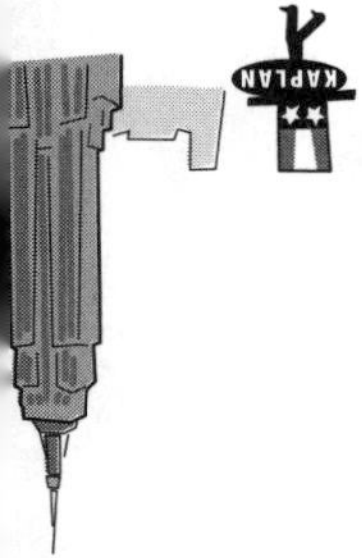

Many cities grew rapidly in area and population beginning in the late 19th century. "New" immigrants from southern and eastern Europe (**#181**) tended to settle in large cities on the east coast. As farms became more mechanized, people sought opportunities in urban areas that were not available in rural regions.

Why important? Cities strained to adjust to rapid growth by providing public transportation and municipal water systems. The trend of Americans leaving rural areas to move to cities continues.

168. JOHN D. ROCKEFELLER

Thirty Years of Change, 1865–1897

The richest mogul and founder of the Standard Oil empire (today's Exxon), Rockefeller was the world's first billionaire. He employed both horizontal and vertical integration (**#170**) in his business practices. His "flow chart" model of business organization is still used today. Like most of the moguls of his age, Rockefeller was attacked for using ruthless business practices to eliminate competition.

Why important? Rockefeller was *the* prototype of an American mogul. His business practices wiped out smaller competitors, but he also gave away almost $500 million to charities.

183. URBAN GROWTH

Thirty Years of Change, 1865–1897

169. SHERMAN ANTITRUST ACT

In 1882, Congress voted to halt all further immigration from China.

Why important? The Chinese Exclusion Act was the first of many laws that attempted to limit immigration into the United States. This particular Act was eventually revoked to some extent.

In 1890, Congress passed this law to attempt to check the power of the growing monopolies in railroads, oil, and banking. It outlawed corporations ("trusts") that became monopolies, as well as "conspiracy in restraint of trade" (moguls getting together to control markets).

Why important? This is another early step toward government regulation of the economy **(#163)**.

182. CHINESE EXCLUSION ACT

Near the end of the 19th century, immigration patterns changed. Millions of immigrants arrived from southern and eastern Europe and from Asia. Up to this time, most immigrants who traveled to America of their own will were from western Europe.

Why important? From 1890 to 1920, almost 20 million immigrants arrived. Most settled into cities on the east coast, creating social and economic changes that had long-term effects.

170. VERTICAL AND HORIZONTAL INTEGRATION

Thirty Years of Change, 1865–1897

The moguls (**#165**) developed these business practices. Horizontal integration means to control one level of production; for example, by the early 1880s Standard Oil controlled 90% of the oil refineries in America. Vertical integration means to possess every level of industrial production, from the iron mines to the trains that hauled ore to the steel mill.

Why important? Wealthy industrialists pursued both strategies to make the production process more efficient and profitable. Businesses today still use them.

181. "NEW" IMMIGRANTS

Thirty Years of Change, 1865–1897

171. GOSPEL OF WEALTH

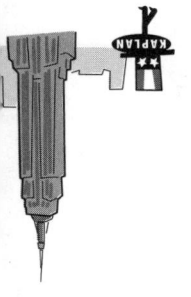

A labor activist for several decades, Debs was jailed for leading the Pullman Strike in 1894. In 1919 the Supreme Court case *Debs v. United States* ruled that court orders that forced striking workers to return to their jobs were constitutional. Debs became a Socialist and ran unsuccessfully for president five times.

Why important? Eugene Debs was an important part of American politics for three decades and was arguably American history's best-known Socialist.

With wealth comes the responsibility to use riches for good. Andrew Carnegie (**#166**) wrote an essay called "The Gospel of Wealth" on this theme, in 1899. This concept was promoted in the Gilded Age (**#154**) by Baptist minister Russell Conwell and adopted by the newly rich industrial leaders of the day. In Conwell's view, God directs money to those who will use it to benefit others. **Why important?** The Gospel of Wealth was a big reason why Carnegie, Morgan, and especially Rockefeller contributed millions of dollars to various causes.

180. EUGENE DEBS

Thirty Years of Change, 1865–1897

172. MAIL-ORDER COMPANIES

Several violent strikes took place in this era, including the Great Railroad Strike of 1877, the Haymarket Riot of 1886, the Homestead Steel Strike of 1892, and the Pullman Strike of 1894.

Why important? Factory owners clearly had the advantage in this period, since none of these strikes benefited workers and hundreds of strikers were killed. Labor unions did not begin to gain equal footing with management until the 1930s.

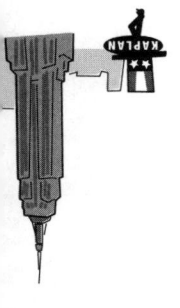

Sears, Roebuck and Company and Montgomery Ward were the two largest distributors of goods to people across the country, especially farmers, in the late 19th century. Almost everything a consumer could imagine was available for delivery through the mail.

Why important? Sears and Ward's were two of the first nationwide merchants. They developed some of the first "department stores" and were a mainstay of American consumer society through the 20th century.

▲ 179. LABOR STRIKES, LATER 19TH CENTURY

Thirty Years of Change, 1865–1897

173. HORATIO ALGER

Samuel Gompers founded the American Federation of Labor (AFL) in 1886 and led it until the 1920s. He pushed for higher wages through collective bargaining. The AFL merged with a rival union, the Congress of Industrial Organizations (**#270**) in 1955.

Why important? The AFL was America's largest labor union at the beginning of the 20th century.

Horatio Alger wrote a series of "rags to riches" books designed to inspire young people in the Gilded Age to work hard and be honest.

Why important? The stories promised the "American dream" of wealth and happiness to millions of young people, and they were especially appealing to immigrants.

---

178. AFL

Thirty Years of Change, 1865–1897

174. INDUSTRIAL TECHNOLOGY OF THE LATER 19TH CENTURY

Terrence Powderly was a prominent leader of this early national labor union. (It was founded in 1869 by Uriah S. Stephens, who led the group until 1879.) The union allowed men and women, blacks and whites to join and promoted labor and social reforms. Membership grew to almost 750,000, but public support declined after the Haymarket riot (**#179**).

Why important? Powderly's willingness to welcome minorities and women into the union was decades ahead of leaders of other unions.

Americans began to lead the world in inventions. Thomas Edison invented the lightbulb (1879), the phonograph (1877), and the movie camera (1891), just to name a few. Alexander Graham Bell invented the telephone (1876). Telegraph cables ran under the Atlantic and Pacific Oceans. An easy-to-use camera, the Kodak, became popular with well-to-do consumers. At the end of the century, automobiles began to hit the streets.

Why important? The great number and variety of inventions developed in this era shows that America was a technological powerhouse.

177. KNIGHTS OF LABOR

Thirty Years of Change, 1865–1897

▼ 175. ECONOMICS OF THE LATER 19TH CENTURY

Thirty Years of Change, 1865–1897

In the 1860s workers first attempted to strengthen their economic power by organizing into unions. Their goals were to increase wages, to shorten the workday, and to make working conditions safer. Factory owners often closed factories (lockouts) and hired strikebreakers (replacements) or private "armies" to break the will of union strikers.

Why important? The earliest unions, such as the National Labor Union, were largely unsuccessful but they provided a template of action for more successful subsequent groups.

Despite some difficulties, the overall economic trend saw wages rise in the latter half of the 19th century. The biggest trend was the increasing size and importance of the middle class. Huge industrial empires arose. In 1873 and 1893, "panics" (depressions) increased unemployment. Farmers made less toward the end of the century than in the 1860s.

Why important? Overall, the economy improved from the Civil War to the end of the century despite serious setbacks.

176. LABOR UNIONS

Thirty Years of Change, 1865–1897

Use the following blank pages to create your own flashcards for additional terms you need to remember. Just write the term on one side and the definition on the other side. You can even flip the book over to make twice as many flashcards!

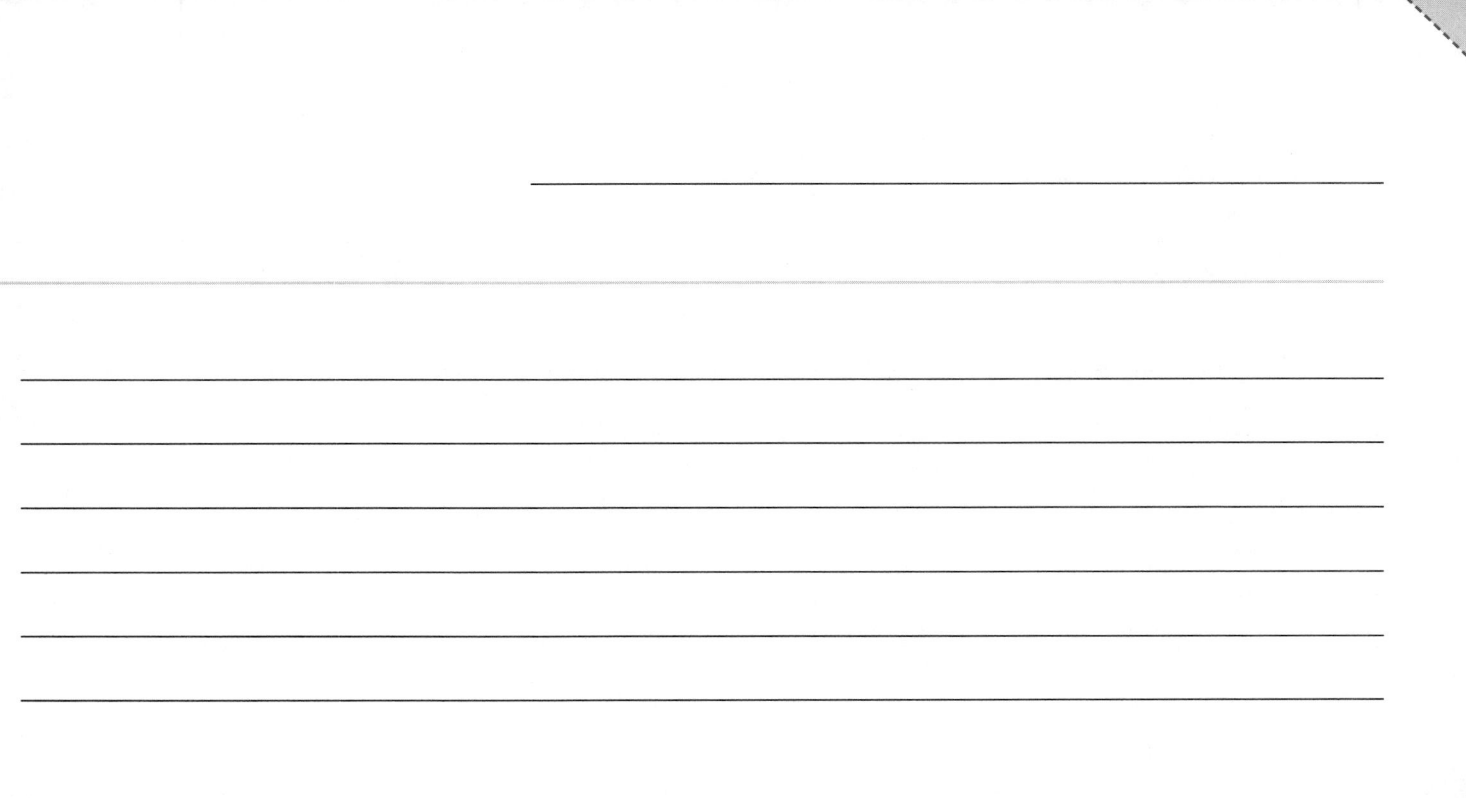

Introducing a smarter way to learn.

- Basic concepts through focused, practice-based learning
- Concepts for everyday life
- Recognition and recall exercises
- Quizzes throughout

KAPLAN

Published by Simon & Schuster

www.kaptest.com

Available wherever books are sold.

Exactly what you need for the AP Exams.

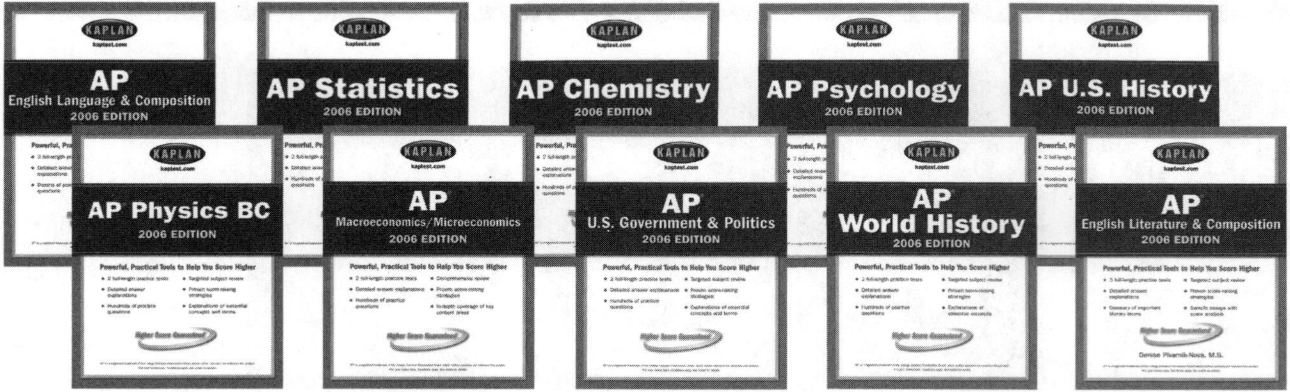

KAPLAN

Available wherever books are sold. **Published by Simon & Schuster** **www.kaptest.com**